Mathematics and Optimal Form

MATHEMATICS AND OPTIMAL FORM

Stefan Hildebrandt

Anthony Tromba

SCIENTIFIC
AMERICAN
LIBRARY

An imprint of Scientific American Books, Inc.
New York

Library of Congress Cataloging in Publication Data

Hildebrandt, Stefan.
  Mathematics and optimal form.

  (Scientific American library)
  Bibliography: p.
  Includes index.
  1. Nature (Aesthetics) 2. Form (Philosophy)
3. Motion. 4. Calculus of variations. 5. Mathematics.
I. Tromba, Anthony. II. Title.
BH301.N3H55 1984   117   84-23461
ISBN 0-7167-5009-0

Printed in the United States of America
Book design by Malcolm Grear Designers
Scientific American Library is published by
Scientific American Books, Inc., a subsidiary
of Scientific American, Inc.

Distributed by W. H. Freeman and Company,
41 Madison Avenue, New York, New York 10010

1 2 3 4 5 6 7 8 9 0 KP 2 1 0 8 9 8 7 6 5 4

In memory of Richard Courant

The Bewitchment

Von Korf finds out his distant cousin is—
            a sorceress
who fashions planets out of herbal fizz;
           and so he hurries, yes,
he hurries there to O-de-lée-de-lizz
           to see the sorceress.

He finds her on a meadow by her home
           and asks her if she be
the one who blows the planets out of foam—
           and if she be the Faërie—
the Faërie from O-de-lée-de-lome?
           Ah, yes, indeed, she be!

She offers him the pitcher and the straw;
           Korf blows,—and from a gleam,
Behold! A wondrous sphere without a flaw
           expands in space supreme,
Expands as if it were a world he saw,
           and not just foam and dream.

Detaching from its stalk, the planet veers
aloft, and gently up,
and blends into the music of the spheres
(a Heavenly Choir), floats up . . .
a strain as from the shepherd's pipe appears . . .
distant tones push up . . .

And in the rounded mirror of this world,
von Korf perceives with zest,
of all the happy things that ever swirled
into his mind, the best,—
his mouth agape, beholds his own fair world,
von Korf, possessed.

He names his cousin "Muse,"—von Korf, possessed,—
But look! Oh, look again!
For something grabs him by the vest
and leads him far awain,
Abducts him out of O-de-lá-de-lest
toward the new domain.

Christian Morgenstern
Translation from the German by Helen and Hans Lewy

CONTENTS

PREFACE

This book is an account of the calculus of variations, an area of mathematics that deals with optimal forms in geometry and nature—with problems of maxima and minima. Starting with the illustrations in the Prologue, we can see remarkably regular forms and patterns in nature. Why does nature produce certain forms and why does it prefer them to other conceivable forms?

Such questions led to the beginning of mathematics about 3,000 years ago. The Greek word *mathema*—which means knowledge, cognition, understanding, perception—suggests that the study of mathematics began with asking questions about the world. The historical sections of our account show that a large part of the development of mathematics was the result of a desire to comprehend nature. Mathematics, however, is more than the handmaiden of other sciences. It is, as Carl Friedrich Gauss stated, irrelevant whether one applies mathematical knowledge to number theory or to the movement of a lump of matter such as a planet. Throughout history, mathematicians have pursued their own ideas, whether relevant to society or not, and have enjoyed the beauty of their discoveries and the challenge of mathematical problems. If the reader finally appreciates mathematics as an integral part of our culture, this book will have achieved its aim.

In this book, we have not used the mathematical formulas and symbols that make modern mathematics so effective and powerful. Indispensable as they are for the working mathematician, extensive training is needed to master mathematical language, a language that may seem strange and alienating to the lay reader. Jonathan Swift ridiculed a society dominated by mathematicians when he described the court of the King of Laputa in *Gulliver's Travels:*

The knowledge I had in mathematics gave me great assistance in acquiring their phraseology, which depended much upon that science and music; and in the latter I was not unskilled. Their ideas are perpetually conversant in lines and figures. If they would, for example, praise the beauty of a woman, or any other animal, they describe it by rhombs, circles, parallelograms, ellipses, and other geometrical terms, or by words of art drawn from music, needless here to repeat. I observed in the king's kitchen all sorts of mathematical and musical instruments, after the figures of which they cut up the joints that were served to his Majesty's table.

We would like to express our thanks to all who have helped us in writing this book: to Brigitte Hildebrandt, for continual support and discussion; to Peter Renz, who suggested this project and provided judicious suggestions as it developed; to our editors, James Maurer and Patricia Mittelstadt, for their careful work; to many friends, colleagues, and referees, for reading and criticizing our manuscript or parts of it, including Maria Athanassenas, Josef Bemelmans, Elizabeth Bernhardt, Emil A. Fellmann, Nellie Friedrichs, Martin Gardner, Marvin Greenberg, Peter Kern, Albrecht Küster, Rolf Leis, Tim Poston, Chen Ning Yang, and Nancy Wingfield; to Cathy Anderson, for patiently checking the proofs; to Helen and Hans Lewy, for providing a congenial translation of Morgenstern's poem "The Bewitchment"; to Egbert Brieskorn and Stephen Smale, for photographs of crystals; to Berthold Burkhardt, Frei Otto, and the collaborators and students at the Institute for Light Weight Structures in Stuttgart, for generously permitting us to use their photographic archive and for assistance and stimulating discussions; to Emil A. Fellmann, for friendly advice and for providing some historical photographs; to Manfred Kage, for his untiring help and permission to select from his archive of photographs; to Michael Meier, for his photograph of the Devil's Post Pile; to Ortwin Wohlrab, for producing computer graphics of minimal surfaces; to Tom Noddy, for the pictures from his show "Bubble Magic"; to Heinz-Otto Peitgen, for providing the "chaos" pictures; to Eric Pitts and Berthold Burkhardt, for preparing photographs of minimal surfaces with free boundaries; to Rolf Lenzen, for referring to a picture of Dido; to Klaus Steffen and Thomas Deussen, for the photographs of minimal-surface systems in the ten possible networks of great circles on the sphere; to Alan Schoen, for permitting us to take photographs of his models of minimal surfaces; to T. G. Wang, for the drawing of the three-lobed rotating drop; and to Paul Concus and

Robert Finn, for the photograph of a liquid in free fall; to the libraries of the universities in Basel, Bonn, Göttingen, and Heidelberg; to the Lick Observatory, the Jet Propulsion Laboratory in Pasadena, the Bildarchiv Preussischer Kulturbesitz in Berlin, the Biblioteca Apostolica Vaticana, the Liebieghaus in Frankfurt/Main, *Scientific American*, LIFE magazine, the Escher Foundation, the Metropolitan Museum in New York, the National Portrait Gallery in London, the Öffentliche Kunstsammlung, Basel, The Herzog Anton Ulrich-Museum Braunschweig for the permission to use their archives and for providing photos; and last but not least to the Sonderforschungsbereich 72 of Bonn University and to the Max Planck Institut für Mathematik, Bonn, for generous and continuous support.

We cannot give credit to all authors from whose work we have drawn our information. With very few exceptions, we have not mentioned the names of contemporary scientists. However, we would never have been able to write this book without the discussions through the years with our friends and colleagues, and we are grateful for their unselfish support.

Stefan Hildebrandt
Anthony Tromba

Bonn, April 30, 1984

Mathematics and Optimal Form

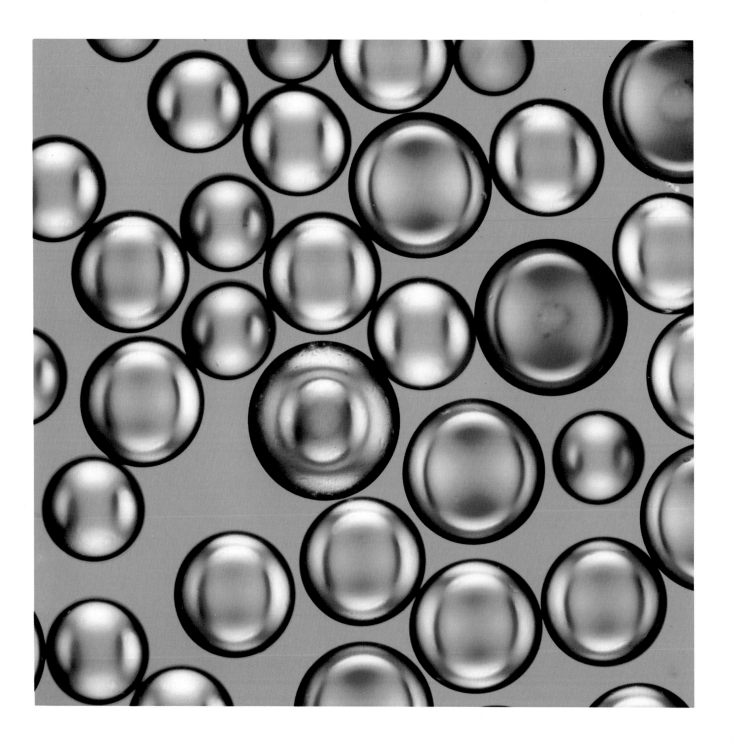

On Form and Shape

Since ancient times, circle and sphere have been considered the perfect forms in geometry. For the Greeks, they were the symbols of the ultimate symmetry of the divine. What could be better suited to the immutable and eternal motion of the planets than circular motion? For this reason, the Greeks believed that the planets in the heavens must move on perfect circles, though these might in turn move on other circles. The Greek philosopher Xenophanes (about 565–470 B.C.) disposed of the multitude of gods of popular belief and replaced them by a unique and supreme God, to whom he attributed the shape of a sphere. Aristotle wrote about the ideas of Xenophanes:

If God is the best of all, then, he claims, there can be only one. For if there are two or even more, then the one cannot anymore be the very best and strongest of all, because each one of the many gods has the same claim to this rank. In fact, godliness and godly power mean superiority, mean to be the best of all, and not to be surpassed. . . . Hence there can only be God, the same from all sides, and everywhere seeing, hearing, and feeling. Otherwise the various parts would be superior and inferior to each other, and this is impossible. Hence such a universal homogeneity of God implies that he has the shape of a sphere. . . . And since God has his existence in everything, uniquely and eternally, and because he is uniformly the same and round as a ball, thus he is neither limited nor unlimited, neither in rest nor in motion.

The spherical form is as appealing today as it was to the Greeks. We admire the perfect roundness of a floating soap bubble blown by a child. Ballotini balls, which are tiny glass balls, have the same immaculate spherical shape. They have long been used in Venetian glass mosaics. Colonies of marvellous spherical symmetry are generated by green

Ballotini balls.

Flagellates are unicellular organisms that move by means of one or more *flagella* (small whips). Some species of flagellates live as solitary individuals; others may form colonies. The volvox algae produce rather sizable colonies; the spherical surface of each colony may contain as many as 20,000 single cells, each carrying a whip. A volvox colony can organize the movement of its whips to enable it to rotate. Truly splendid spheres are generated by the species *Volvox aureus*, a type of oceanic plankton.

A montage of Jupiter with four of its moons. Io is nearest to Jupiter; next comes Europa, then Ganymede, and Callisto. These satellites were discovered by Galileo. Besides these four, at least ten other, much smaller moons circle Jupiter; a faint ring of particles also surrounds it.

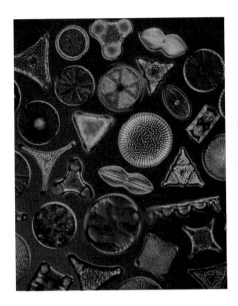

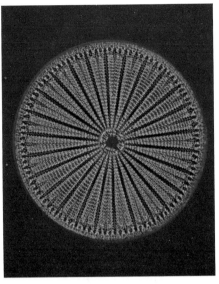

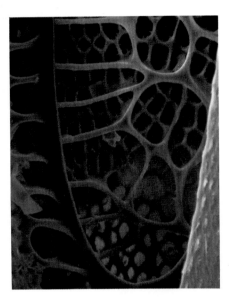

Diatom skeletons, each of which is like a box, with a bottom and a cover.

The species *Arachnoidiscus USA* creates a beautiful disc shell, which might very well serve as the pattern for a gothic rose window.

The electron microscope reveals the filigreed network of the struts and arches of a diatom, which is penetrated by the living protoplasm.

flagellates of the genus *Volvox*. Similarly, the planets of our solar system and their satellites are of nearly spherical shape.

The forces that produce spheres can also produce the shapes seen in the accompanying photographs of diatoms, one-celled algae, which are classic objects of microscopy. They are bounded by a silicious armor of various delicate geometric shapes.

A great variety of marvelous forms in nature are produced by soap films and bubbles. For reasons we will see later, three soap films will always (if free to do so) form angles of 120° to each other, whether they are spanning wire frames or sitting between glass plates.

The photograph at the upper right on the next page is a view of soap films suspended between two parallel glass plates. Because we are seeing the films as straight lines, it is evident that we are looking at their edges, which means that the films meet each plate at a right angle. Such right angles are formed whenever soap films are allowed to arrange their boundaries freely on a supporting surface. For example, the soap films form angles of 90° with the sides of a metal strip seen on edge as a thick black line in the lower photograph. Among themselves, however, they meet at 120° angles.

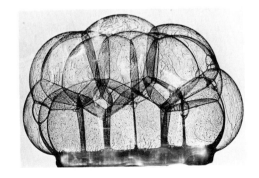

A float of bubbles.

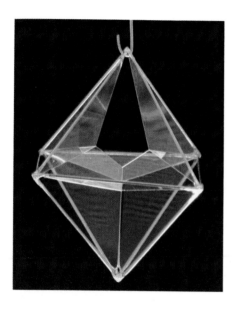

A system of soap films bounded by the
twelve edges of an octahedron.

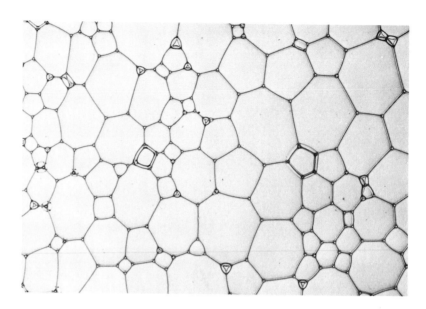

Soap films between two parallel glass plates.
Notice the typical Y-form wherever three
films meet. Some cells are bounded by curved
films; the bulge is caused by a pressure difference between adjacent cells.

Soap films between two parallel glass plates
form 90° angles along a surface (dark line).

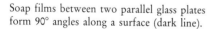

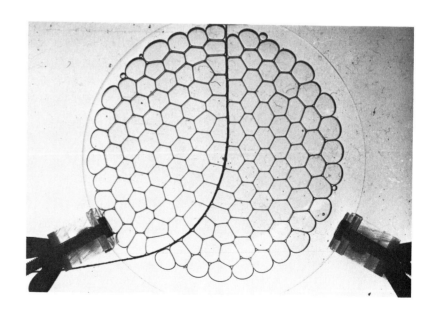

The Y-shaped linkage seen in soap films is often found in nature and can cause repeating hexagonal patterns, as in these beehive cells.

An examination of insect wings and beehive cells reveals their similarity to soap films. It is also fascinating to see the similarities between certain systems of soap films that span polyhedral frames and some unicellular creatures called radiolarians.

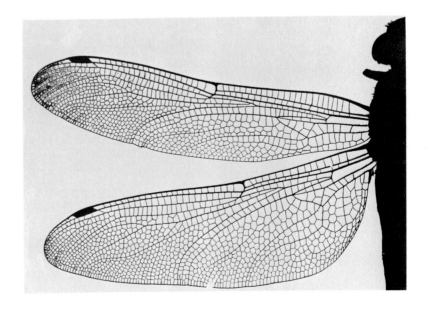

Insect wings may resemble soap films.

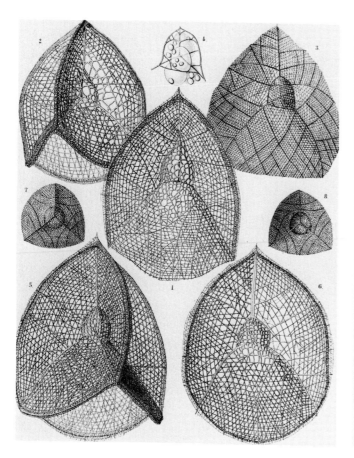

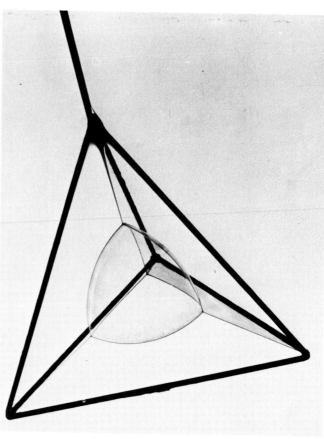

Drawings by the German biologist Ernst Haeckel of skeletons of the radiolarian called *Callimitra*. Its shape resembles that of a system of six flat soap films holding a bubble, all suspended within a tetrahedral framework.

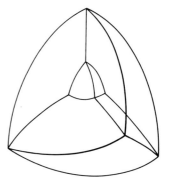

A living radiolarian. Haeckel described or depicted 4,314 species and 739 genera of these minute creatures.

The skeleton of a radiolarian.

A phenomenon closely related to soap films and soap bubbles is the formation of a drop, which also kindles our imagination, reminding us of the lovely image of sunlit dew on the petals of a flower.

So sweet a kiss the golden sun gives not
To those fresh morning drops upon the rose,

wrote Shakespeare in *Love's Labor's Lost*.

Water droplet, with refraction halo.

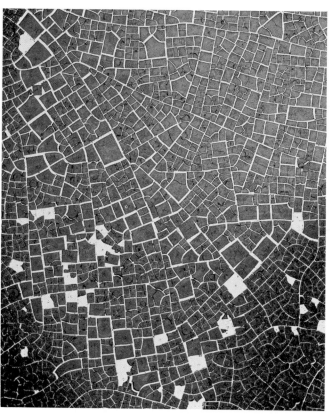

Is this an aerial photograph of farmland? No, it is of fissures in a gelatinous preparation of tin oil.

Yet phenomena that stir unpleasant thoughts and feelings, such as cracks, fissures, and crevasses in ice or in drying mud, may also show patterns quite similar to those created by soap films. Whether we see 90° or 120° angles at the points at which the cracks join depends on the material.

Finally, let us consider two dynamical phenomena, the orbits of stars in the heavens and of elementary particles in an accelerator. These phenomena are described by the phase portrait of a Hamiltonian flow. Such a flow is pictured on the next page. It is difficult to visualize without the aid of a computer.

Devil's Post Pile.

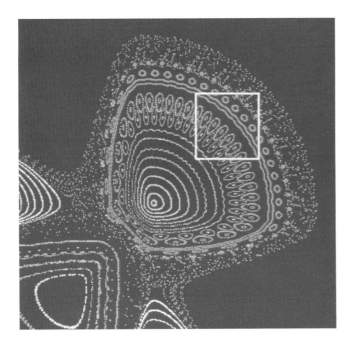

A computer-generated phase portrait of a Hamiltonian flow.

Detail of the square in the adjacent phase portrait.

Having viewed some of the stunning configurations produced by nature, let us consider this passage from an ancient Buddhist writing:

> . . . a Bodhisattva in accordance with truth knows that form is nothing but holes and cracks, and is indeed like a mass of bubbles, with a nature that has no hardness or solidity.

Holes and cracks and bubbles: is that all there is to nature's design? Whether or not this is so, in looking at the world around us we often do notice a symmetry of form or a regularity of pattern: there seems to be a certain order in chaos. This order suggests that we ought to look for some simple *universal laws* behind the formation of these configurations. Why does nature prefer this or that form to all other conceivable forms? Why do the celestial bodies look like balls, and not like cubes or pyramids? (Nature does not abhor polyhedral configurations such as cubes and pyramids, as we know from crystalline formations.) Why, we may further ask, are the oil drops floating on your broth circular, and not triangular (like some of the diatoms)?

We do not really hope to find a final answer to such questions: very likely there is none. Most scientists have given up the hope of ever finding a complete answer, an ultimate truth. Instead, they content themselves with unraveling a few principles that will enable them, in a given situation, to predict what forms are preferred by nature over others. This modest approach to understanding complex problems has led to much scientific progress.

Throughout history, people have tried to discover such principles, and it is fascinating to see how our understanding of nature has grown by means of this process. Theory after theory has been devised in order to comprehend nature. Albert Einstein pointed out two reasons why scientific theories are developed:

> New theories are first of all necessary when we encounter new facts which cannot be "explained" by existing theories. But this motivation for setting up new theories is, so to speak, trivial, imposed from without. There is another, more subtle motive of no less importance. This is the striving toward unification and simplification of the premises of the theory as a whole.

The striving for simplicity corresponds to an ideal that most artists, craftsmen, engineers, and scientists have: What you can do, you can do simply. On the surface, this "principle of the economy of means" is merely an aesthetic concept, resting on the conviction that what is done simply is thus done best; yet it also leads to the idea that nature proceeds in the simplest, most efficient way.

Aluminum crystals.

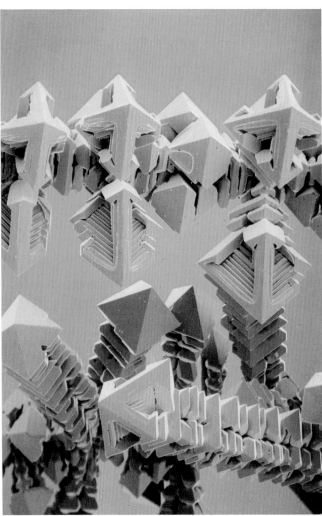

Palladium crystals.

Einstein also commented on the human desire to comprehend nature by means of simple, appealing concepts that relate our perception of nature to logical systems of thought:

There exists a passion for comprehension just as there exists a passion for music. That passion is rather common in children, but gets lost in most people later on. Without this passion, there would be neither mathematics nor natural science. Time and again the passion for understanding has led to the illusion that man is able to comprehend the objective world rationally, by pure thought, without any empirical foundations—in short, by metaphysics. I believe that every true theorist is a kind of tamed metaphysicist, no matter how pure a "positivist" he may fancy himself. The metaphysicist believes that the logically simple is also the real. The tamed metaphysicist believes that not all that is logically simple is embodied in experienced reality, but that the totality of all sensory experience can be "comprehended" on the basis of a conceptual system built on premises of great simplicity. The skeptic will say that this is a "miracle creed." Admittedly so, but it is a miracle creed which has been borne out to an amazing extent by the development of science.

To no one's surprise, mathematics has played and continues to play a prominent role in the development of such conceptual systems. It appears to be the only tool that allows us to formulate and exploit with precision our insights into the phenomena of the physical world. The British physicist P. A. M. Dirac has expressed this fact in the following way:

It seems to be one of the fundamental features of nature that fundamental physical laws are described in terms of a mathematical theory of great beauty and power, needing quite a high standard of mathematics for one to understand it. You may wonder: Why is nature constructed along these lines? One can only answer that our present knowledge seems to show that nature is so constructed. We simply have to accept it. One could perhaps describe the situation by saying that God is a mathematician of a very high order, and He used very advanced mathematics in constructing the universe. Our feeble attempts at mathematics enable us to understand a bit of the universe, and as we proceed to develop higher and higher mathematics we can hope to understand the universe better.

In this book we shall consider some of the theories that claim to explain form and motion in our world. We shall see how they came about and what role mathematics has played in their development. In particular, we shall emphasize the *principle of the economy of means*, which throughout the centuries has served as a major tool for comprehending physical phenomena. Our goal will be to find a link between mathematics and physics that is easy to understand. The mathematical theory that provides this link is called the *calculus of variations*. Its foundations were laid, and its connection to physics was conceived, during the period of the Baroque and the Rococo, from the end of the seventeenth century through the eighteenth century—that is, at the very beginning of the development of modern science. We shall therefore start our account by considering some of the mathematical and philosophical ideas of that time.

1

The Grand Scheme of the World

All that is superfluous displeases God and nature.
All that displeases God and nature is evil.

(Dante Alighieri, about 1300)

Throughout history, people have searched for laws to describe the phenomena of our physical world. However, no general principle, encompassing all phenomena, was proposed until 1744, when the French scientist Pierre-Louis Moreau de Maupertuis put forth his grand scheme of the universe, which became known as the *law of least action*. He published an elaborated version of his ideas in 1746 as "The laws of motion and of rest deduced from a metaphysical principle."

Action and Economy in Nature: Maupertuis's Principle

The "metaphysical principle" of Maupertuis is the assumption that nature always operates with the greatest possible economy. For example, in a homogeneous medium, light would take the shortest possible path. From this idea, he drew the following conclusion, which he stated as his *general principle*:

If there occurs some change in nature, the amount of action necessary for this change must be as small as possible.

Pierre-Louis Moreau de Maupertuis (1698–1759), in Northern costume commemorating his Arctic expedition.

What is this "action" that nature is supposed to consume so thriftily?

Think of your mailman, and consider how to describe his action.

If he travels 2 kilometers in 1 hour, you would say that he has carried out twice as much "action" as he would in traveling 2 kilometers in 2 hours. However, you would also say that he carries out twice as much "action" in traveling 2 kilometers in 2 hours than in traveling 1 kilometer in 1 hour. Altogether then, your mailman, by traveling 2 kilometers in 1 hour carries out *four* times as much "action" as he would in traveling 1 kilometer in 1 hour.

We shall, using this intuitive idea, define action as the product of distance, velocity, and mass:

$$action = mass \times distance \times velocity.$$

Mass is included in this definition to account for the mailman's bag. Moreover, according to Leibniz, the kinetic energy E is given by the formula

$$E = \tfrac{1}{2} \times mass \times (velocity)^2;$$

so action has the same physical dimension as

$$energy \times time,$$

because velocity is distance divided by time. Thus we have arrived at a quantitative definition of action, which we need to have if we want to give a mathematical formulation of a law of nature that uses the concept of "action." It is this formula for action that was used by Maupertuis.* We may paraphrase Maupertuis's principle as

Nature always minimizes action.

Maupertuis saw in this principle an expression of the wisdom of the Supreme Being, of God, according to which everything in nature is performed in the most economical way. He wrote, "*What satisfaction for the human spirit that, in contemplating these laws which contain the*

That is, if weather excluded [handwritten margin note]

---

*It had already been stated by Leibniz, who, by the way, had used very similar reasoning to define the concept of action. Very likely Maupertuis heard about this from one of the Bernoulli family, a dynasty of Swiss mathematicians who, beginning in the first half of the eighteenth century, made the city of Basel a world center of mathematics.

principle of motion and of rest for all bodies in the universe, he finds the proof of existence of Him who governs the world."

You are probably waiting to see how the action principle can be used to explain the beautiful forms and patterns created by nature encountered in the Prologue. However, we must ask you to be patient, until we have covered enough background material to enable you to understand the mathematical treatment of optimum problems. For the moment, we would like to explore the philosophical and scientific ideas which at the time led to the law of least action. How was Maupertuis led to the concept that nature operates with minimal action? Isn't this more a principle of good housekeeping by the Creator than a basis for exact science? It is indeed very interesting to see how this moral principle entered physics. To this end, we shall turn to the late Baroque, when the fundamental mathematical and physical ideas about which we are writing arose. We will see how at that time philosophical, mathematical, and physical concepts developed and merged into a great scheme of the universe that is epitomized in the law of least action. Simultaneously, we will have a glimpse at a fascinating period of history.

Preestablished Harmony: The Philosophy of Leibniz

One of the most influential men of the Baroque era was Gottfried Wilhelm Leibniz, diplomat, philosopher, mathematician, scientist, and universal scholar. His philosophical ideas were presented in his *Essais de Théodicée sur la bonté de Dieu, la liberté de l'homme et l'origine du mal* (Essays on theodicy: On the kindness of God, the freedom of man, and the origin of evil), which appeared in 1710. There he developed the philosophical idea that our world is organized to be *the best of all possible worlds*. This philosophy, well known in educated circles during the first half of the eighteenth century, had many supporters. The most influential of them was probably the German philosopher Christian Wolff (1679–1754). Maupertuis was certainly influenced by Leibniz, although his basic philosophical views differed considerably from those of the great scholar.

Let us look at some of Leibniz's ideas. He had occupied himself in his *Théodicée* with considering how the assumption of an almighty, omniscient, and infinitely good Creator could be compatible with the imperfection of his creation.

Gottfried Wilhelm Leibniz (1646–1716).

By very much simplifying it, we may describe Leibniz's theory as follows. God does not interfere, like a clumsy clockmaker, from time to time with the affairs of this world, to regulate the hands of His clock. On the contrary, God created His world in preestablished harmony. Like a skillful clockmaker looking after his clockwork, God brought the nature of each single part of His world for all eternity into agreement with the nature of all the others. Thus all parts are forever in complete harmony with each other. This alone is worthy of God, the most intelligent and almighty being.

And God exists, according to Leibniz, for the following reason: God is that being who possesses all properties to the highest degree, insofar as these properties can coexist. This condition is necessary, because some properties, such as holiness and omnipotence, cannot totally coexist. The holiness of God restricts His omnipotence, since it is incompatible with His holiness to do the evil that He could do by means of His omnipotence. Therefore it follows that God may indeed think of all possible worlds, but he may want and, hence, may create only the best among them: the best of all possible worlds.

Thus the existence of this world as best of all possible worlds is a consequence of the existence of God. Accordingly, any other world would necessarily be less complete than ours; yet the existence of many evils and insufficiencies is not denied: sin and evil do exist. Moreover, Leibniz proves that a world without sin and evil would be impossible.

The best possible world is created in such a way that a preestablished harmony exists between freedom and necessity, between the grace of God and the realm of nature. God as Architect of the world, and God as Lord of the universe, are in perfect agreement. Leibniz understood perfectly well that this world, being merely the best selection out of what is possible, may be much worse than what we might hope for. However, popular misunderstandings of Leibniz's views reduced his thoughts to this oversimplification: All that exists is good.

If you don't feel that our world is in very good shape, you share the opinion of several contemporaries of Leibniz, and certainly that of Voltaire, the French philosopher, who in 1758 wrote a malicious satire of Leibniz's philosophy titled *Candide, ou l'Optimisme*. It was an immediate sensational success in Europe, and within 20 years forty-two editions appeared. The main characters of the book are the philosopher Pangloss, tutor of the young baroness Cunegonde at the castle of Baron Thunder-ten-tronckh in Westphalia, and his faithful pupil Candide, an illegitimate member of this noble family. These three people experience some rather startling adventures. But let us turn to Voltaire:

Voltaire (1694–1778).

Pangloss taught metaphysico-theologico-cosmolonicology. He proved incontestably that there is no effect without cause, and that in this best of all possible worlds, his lordship's country seat was the most beautiful of mansions and her ladyship the best of all possible ladyships.

"It is proved," he used to say, "that things cannot be other than they are, for since everything was made for a purpose, it follows that everything is made for the best purpose. Observe: our noses were made to carry spectacles; so we have spectacles. Legs were clearly intended for breeches, and so we wear them. Stones were meant for carving and for building houses, and that is why my lord has a most beautiful house; for the greatest baron in Westphalia ought to have the noblest residence. And since pigs were made to be eaten, we eat pork all year around. It follows that those who maintain that all is right talk nonsense; they ought to say, all is for the best."

The events that then follow do not strengthen our trust in these assertions of Pangloss, as is to be expected. Candide is kicked out of the castle when Cunegonde wants to experience with him the interplay between cause and effect, and subsequently gets into the Bulgarian army, where he survives the horrors of a battle between the Bulgars and the Abars (who stand for the Prussians and the French).

Investigating the interplay of cause and effect at Castle Thunder-ten-tronckh.

Those who have never seen two well-trained armies drawn up for battle can have no idea of the beauty and brilliance of the display. Bugles, fifes, oboes, drums, and salvoes of artillery produced such harmony as Hell itself could not rival. The opening barrage destroyed about six thousand men on each side. Rifle fire that followed rid this best of worlds of about nine or ten thousand villains who infested its surface. Finally, the bayonet provided "sufficient reason" for the death of several thousand more. The total casualties amounted to about thirty thousand. Candide trembled like a philosopher, and hid himself as best he could during this heroic butchery.

When all was over, and the rival kings were celebrating their victory with Te Deums in their respective camps, Candide decided to find somewhere else to pursue his reasoning into cause and effect. He picked his way over piles of the dead and the dying, and reached a neighboring village on the Abar side of the border. It was now no more than a smoking ruin, for the Bulgars had burned it to the ground in accordance with the terms of international law.

Disaster is followed by disaster: Castle Thunder-ten-tronckh is destroyed, its inhabitants murdered or driven away. Cunegonde ends as a lady of easy virtue in Lisbon, where, having been shipwrecked, Candide and Pangloss arrive just in time to experience the terrible earthquake of October 1, 1755. Thirty thousand men, women, and children were crushed to death under the ruins.

The following day, while creeping amongst the ruins Candide and Pangloss found something to eat. . . . Some of the citizens whom they had helped gave them as good a dinner as could be managed after such a disaster. The meal was certainly a sad affair, and the guests wept as they ate; but Pangloss consoled them with the assurance that things could not be otherwise:

"For all this," said he, "is a manifestation of the rightness of things, since if there is a volcano at Lisbon it could not be anywhere else. For it is impossible for things not to be where they are, because everything is for the best."

In 1762, three years after its first appearance, *Candide* was placed on the papal Index. However, Voltaire had been careful to publish it under a pseudonym, and, as all Europe laughed, he denied vehemently that he was its author.

It is remarkable that, at least initially, the principle of least action shared the fate of its philosophical forebear. The period following its introduction resembled a full-fledged tragicomedy, as once again, to the great amusement of Europe, Voltaire shot off his verbal barbs, this time directed against Maupertuis, for whom the result was disastrous. However, before we turn to this part of our story, we want to describe in very general terms the mathematics on which the principle of least action was to be built.

The Beginning of the Calculus of Variations

In the last third of the seventeenth century, there had been an important development in mathematics. Newton and Leibniz had each independently created the infinitesimal calculus, which is the mathematical foundation of modern science. Soon after this new tool had become available, another new discipline, based on the first calculus, was developed; it was later called "the calculus of variations." The founding fathers of this new field were three world-famous Swiss scientists, all from the city of Basel: the brothers Johann and Jakob Bernoulli, and Johann's student Leonhard Euler, who would become the most celebrated mathematician of the eighteenth century.

The goals of this new mathematical discipline are closely related to the philosophical ideas just described. They are to find mathematical descriptions of optimal objects and to develop the mathematical techniques needed to find them.

Obviously, mathematicians are interested in such problems. In daily life, we must regularly decide such questions as which situation is "best" or "worst"; which object has some property to a "highest" or "lowest" degree; what is the "optimal" strategy to maximize pleasure, success, or profit, or to minimize discomfort, failure, or losses? What

Johann Bernoulli (1667–1748). Jakob Bernoulli (1654–1705).

shape for a car will, for a prescribed interior volume, minimize its resistance to air? What shape for a hull will produce the fastest ship? What form for a house has the least possible surface area for a given interior volume, to insure that the least possible heat is lost to the outside? (The answer to this last question can help reduce your heating bill. The Eskimos found it a long time ago: the optimal house form is the igloo—that is, the hemisphere.)

The calculus of variations was developed by the Bernoullis, by Euler, and by the great French mathematician J. L. Lagrange to attack such questions in a systematic way. The basic idea of this mathematical theory is easy to grasp.

Suppose that you are in a mountainous area in the dark. You want to locate the summits but are equipped with only a small flashlight and a water level. How would you proceed? You might walk around and use your water level to try to locate all the places where the ground is horizontal—that is, has a horizontal tangent plane. If the mountain range is geologically very old, so that the surface of the earth is smooth, and not all rock and full of peaks, you can, in principle, find all the summits in this way. However, you may also find other points with horizontal tangent planes—for example, the mountain passes or mountain pits, all of which you might pass on your way to a summit. *In practice*, no one would proceed in this manner; but these considerations show how you could solve this problem *in principle*, by employing the idea of the horizontal tangent. This is how the mathematician locates maxima and minima, by first reducing questions of best or worst, maxima or minima, to a geometric question of finding summits or pits in some mathematically constructed mountain range.* The mathematician then uses a strategy (such as the one described) to focus attention on a small number of points suspected to be maxima (peaks) or minima (pits). This procedure is similar to that of a detective, who uses all available circumstantial evidence to reduce the number of suspects who might have committed a crime. The mathematician establishes a system of differential equations (called the Euler-Lagrange equations) that must be satisfied by the optimal objects that are being sought and then attempts to solve them. Finding the solution is usually difficult, but we will not go into those technical details here.

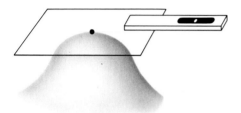

How to find summits using a water level.

Joseph Louis Lagrange (1736–1813).

---

*This is usually a "higher-dimensional" mountain range, that is, one with more than three dimensions. Even though higher-dimensional landscapes cannot be visualized, it is mathematically easy to work with spaces of 4, 10, 47, 1001, or even an infinite number of dimensions.

Peaks, pits, and passes.

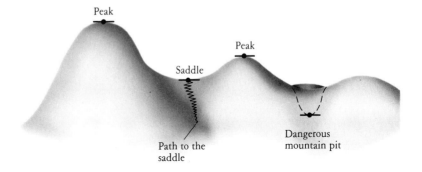

Peak

Peak

Saddle

Path to the
saddle

Dangerous
mountain pit

The Mechanics of Newton

So far, we have described only the philosophical and mathematical ideas from which the principle of least action originated. However, in the form proposed by Maupertuis, the principle was too vaguely formulated to be applied to difficult problems. Euler and Lagrange elaborated and perfected it into a powerful tool that was to become indispensable for physics. An elegant general version appeared in Lagrange's much admired masterpiece, *Mécanique analytique* (Analytical mechanics), which was published in 1788, just one year before the outbreak of the French revolution.

All these developments, however, were based on the revolution in physics that took place when Newton's epoch-making *Philosophiae Naturalis Principia Mathematica* (Mathematical principles of the philosophy of nature) appeared in 1687. This treatise, one of the most influential creations of the human mind, and the foundation of modern physics, is also the solid pillar on which the least-action principle safely rests.

However, Newton's revolutionary ideas were not readily accepted on the continent of Europe, particularly in France, the cultural center of Europe at that time. During the seventeenth century, and until about 1730, continental Europe was dominated by the physical theories of René Descartes. Since the triumph of Newtonian physics, however, they have been almost completely forgotten. The Cartesians, as the followers of Descartes were called, vigorously battled Newtonianism, until the French Academy of Sciences agreed to decide the

René Descartes (1596–1650).

Exaggerated drawings of (*A*) Newton's view of the Earth; (*B*) Descartes's view of the Earth.

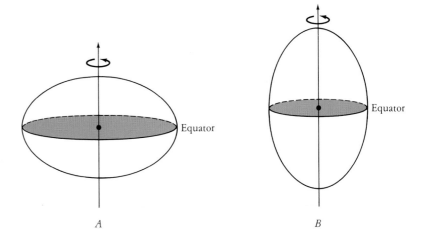

A   *B*

controversy on the basis of facts rather than by debate. It sent out two expeditions, one to the Arctic Circle in Sweden and one to the equator, to take geodesic measurements that would decide whether the Earth was flattened at the poles, as Newton had predicted from his theory of gravitation, or at the equator, as the Cartesians had asserted.

The expedition to the north was carried out in 1736/37 by Maupertuis, who had been an early supporter of the ideas of Newton. From the geodesic measurements taken in Lappland, it could be proved that the Earth was flattened at the poles and that Newton was right. This result was confirmed in 1745 by another expedition led by La Condamine.

The great success of his expedition brought Maupertuis instant renown—a fame that was embellished by the two young Lapp girls whom he had brought back to Paris. Evidently they made quite an impression on the Parisians.

Voltaire, with his prodigious pen and his quick mind, helped to publicize Newton's great triumph. He congratulated Maupertuis for successfully and simultaneously flattening the globe and the Cassinis (well-known astronomers in Paris, and vigorous defenders of the Cartesian view of the Earth's shape). Look once more at Maupertuis's gesture in the figure on page 14, to see how proudly he indicates his success.

Thus the way was cleared for Newtonian physics and for its elegant formulation in terms of variational (optimum) principles. The era of "analytical mechanics" could begin. This is what eventually happened.

The Berlin Controversy over Maupertuis's Principle

In 1740 Frederic II became King of Prussia, the northeastern part of Germany with Berlin as its capital. He wanted to revive the Academy of Sciences in Berlin and invited Voltaire to accept its presidency. Voltaire was pleased but declined to come because he preferred to stay at the domicile of his lady-love, the Marquise du Chatelet.* Frederic therefore offered the presidency of the Prussian academy to Maupertuis, then famous as the organizer of the expedition to the Arctic Circle. He accepted, but did not assume his position until 1746.

Meanwhile, Euler had already come to Berlin in 1741 from St. Petersburg in Russia to become the director of the mathematical-physical section of the Academy. He held this position until 1766, when he returned to St. Petersburg as a member of the Imperial Russian Academy of Sciences. Euler is considered to be the father of Russian mathematics.

By 1744, Euler had already rigorously proved that the least-action principle could be used to describe the motion of a point-mass in a conservative field of forces, such as the motion of a planet around the Sun, and had expressed his conviction that, behind every phenomenon in our universe, we can find a maximum or minimum rule. This result appeared in an appendix to his *Methodus Inveniendi Lineas Curvas Maximi Minimive Proprietate Gaudentes* (A method to find curved lines that enjoy a maximum or minimum property), the first textbook on the calculus of variations and one of the most celebrated books in the history of mathematics. It is certain that Euler had known nothing of Maupertuis's principle when he wrote the appendix to his book in 1743. Moreover, the problems treated by Euler were much more difficult than those that Maupertuis would handle in his 1746 paper.

When, in 1746, Maupertuis published his paper on the least-action principle, he was well aware of Euler's achievement, since he briefly described it in the preface to his publication. Then, however, he added the comment, *"This remark . . . is a beautiful application of my*

---

*This remarkable woman had been tutored by some of the outstanding scientists of her time, including J. S. König and A. C. Clairaut. She prepared, with the assistance of Clairaut, the first and only French translation of Newton's *Principia*, to which Voltaire added upon her death in 1749 a historical preface and a poem, "Sur la Physique de Newton."

principle to the movement of the planets," and thus claimed the right of priority for himself.

Euler reacted by attributing the whole priority to Maupertuis, arguing that his own principle of economy was only an *"a posteriori* insight,"* whereas Maupertuis's law was an *"a priori* conception of the world."* Euler has been criticized strongly for this act. Some historians have attributed it to generosity and loyalty to the president of his academy; others have seen it as a pitiful example of moral weakness. Still other commentators feel that either judgment is too simpleminded and that the real reason for Euler's behavior lies in his philosophical attitude. It is not a question on which certainty is possible.

However, Maupertuis's reasoning had several flaws. First, he supported his principle by only a few examples; second, and worse, the principle was not always correct.

Let us take one of Maupertuis's examples, the reflection of light. Here the law of least action turns out to be equivalent to the rule that light propagates along rays in such a way that the time needed by the light to get from the source to the observer is less than that which would be required along all other possible paths. (This latter rule for light propagation had already been formulated by Fermat in 1662.) If light travels in a homogenenous isotropic medium, like water or air of the same density, this minimum principle amounts to the still simpler rule that the light path is the shortest possible connection of source and observer, a rule already known by the ancient Greeks.

Consider a spherical mirror in such a perfect medium and a ray starting at the center, *M,* of the mirror, as shown on the facing page. The ray, according to Maupertuis's principle, is reflected and travels to some point *P* beyond *M.* It is easy to see that any other path that consists of two straight segments leading from *M* to the mirror and then to *P* is shorter than the light ray. If, on the other hand, we reflect light from a convex mirror, the path of light is indeed minimal. Thus whether nature acts thriftily or wastefully depends only on the shape of the mirror.

With arguments of this kind, the Chevalier d'Arcy showed in 1749 and in 1752 that Maupertuis's principle was not clearly formulated and, moreover, led to incorrect assertions. The theologic-philosophical construction built on the principle of greatest economy was irreparably damaged.

In Berlin, Maupertuis was criticized by a new member of the Academy, the Swiss mathematician Johann Samuel König (1712–1757), who arrived in Berlin in 1750 and claimed that Leibniz had discovered the least-action principle in 1707. A heated controversy

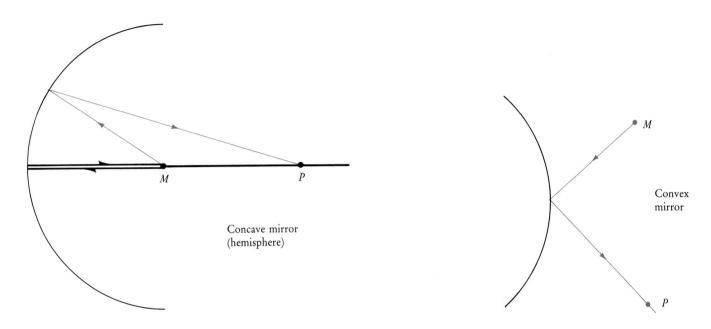

Concave mirror
(hemisphere)

Convex
mirror

Left: Light reflected from a concave surface. The blue lines show a possible connection of *M* with *P* by way of the mirror that is shorter than the actual light ray (as indicated by the heavy black lines). Right: Light reflected from a convex surface.

arose over whether König's documents to support this claim were forged. On April 13, 1752, the Academy declared König's copy of the crucial letter by Leibniz to be a falsification. König reacted by resigning his membership in the Academy, and a heated quarrel started between König, on the one hand, and Maupertuis and Euler, on the other. Voltaire then entered the fray, and in 1752 he attacked Maupertuis in his *Diatribe of Doctor Akakia*. As a result, the literati and encyclopedists of Paris took sides with Voltaire against Maupertuis, and Maupertuis was finished. A sick man, he left King Frederic's court in 1753 to recover his health. Only occasionally did he return to Berlin. He died in 1759 in the city of Basel at the house of his friend Johann II Bernoulli.

Today the dispute about who first discovered the least-action principle is meaningless, as are most quarrels of this kind. We can give both Euler and Maupertuis credit for its discovery. Certainly it was Maupertuis who proposed it as a universal law of physics, from which all other laws should follow, whereas Euler created the mathematical structure that served as model for all later variational principles.

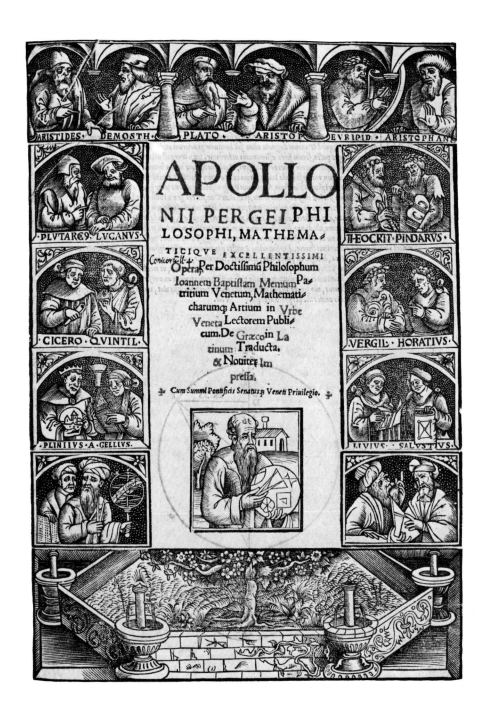

ARISTIDES. DEMOSTH. PLATO. ARISTOT. EVRIPID. ARISTOPHAN.

PLVTARC9. LVCANVS.

THEOCRIT. PINDARVS.

APOLLO
NII PERGEI PHI
LOSOPHI, MATHEMA,
TICIQVE EXCELLENTISSIMI
Conicov sc.li. 4. Opera, Per Doctissimũ Philosophum
Ioannem Baptistam Memum Pa
tritium Venetum, Mathemati
charumꝗ Artium in Vrbe
Veneta Lectorem Publi
cum. De Græco in La
tinum Traducta.
& Nouiter Im
pressa.

Cum Summi Pontificis Senatusꝗ Veneti Priuilegio.

CICERO. QVINTIL.

VERGIL. HORATIVS.

PLINIIVS. A. GELLIVS.

LIVIVS. SALVSTIVS.

2

The Heritage of Ancient Science

Thou, Nature, art my goddess;
To thy laws my services are bound.

(Shakespeare, *King Lear*,
Act I, Scene II, as quoted by Gauss)

Many fundamental ideas in science were conceived in antiquity, and our present way of thinking owes, without doubt, a great deal to our predecessors. One essential idea that modern science has inherited from the classical world is the concept of a fundamental order and harmony to the universe, a harmony that could be reflected in the beauty of mathematical structures. Because Greek mathematics was mainly restricted to geometry, the ancient scientists used geometric models to describe nature.

Interestingly optimum principles appeared in ancient science, but only marginally, although it should have been very pleasing for the ancient scholars to think that the harmony of things corresponds to an optimal order in our world. Let us take a closer look at ancient Greece, and begin to see how the geometry of ideal forms was invented.

Circles, Cycloids, Conic Sections, and the Music of the Spheres

It is usually said that mathematics developed in Greece in the seventh and sixth centuries B.C., after the Greeks had devised a more or less uniform alphabet (the classical Greek alphabet was com-

Frontispiece of Apollonius's *Opera.*

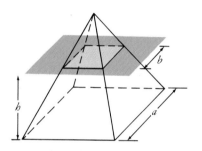

Volume of a frustum of a pyramid with a
square base. $V = \frac{1}{3}h(a^2 + ab + b^2)$.

monly accepted only during the fourth century B.C.). However, modern historians admit that our knowledge about the science of this time is by no means well founded. Primary sources do not exist, and all events were recorded only long after they had actually occurred. Even the scientists of antiquity had no sure knowledge of the origin of mathematics and of the first mathematicians. The traditional stories about the two towering figures of early mathematics, Thales of Miletus (about 624–548 B.C.) and Pythagoras of Samos (about 580–500 B.C.) are probably more or less legendary. It now appears certain that the mathematical knowledge commonly ascribed to the early Greek philosophers was, in fact, known to the Egyptians and the Babylonians many centuries before the rise of Greek civilization. However, the Greeks, who settled throughout the Mediterranean region, must have played an important role in preserving and spreading this knowledge. It is likely that the first major advance that the Greeks made was to consider mathematical concepts (such as numbers and geometric figures) to be abstractions, creations of the human mind, and not part of the real world. A line was no longer considered to be a taut rope or the edge of a pyramid, and a rectangle was not the boundary of a plot of land. Instead, they were defined as ideas, which physical objects could only approximate. It seems quite certain that the Greek philosophers were the first to realize that a mathematical statement must be proved by logical deduction from certain basic facts or axioms. Before, mathematical results had been verified by induction—that is, by sufficient experience. It was a most important advance to realize that a mathematical proposition cannot be proved by a thousand or even a million cases in which it is true, if, in principle, infinitely many cases may occur.

Thales is given credit for having invented the rigorous mathematical proof. Whether he did or not, it was surely clear to the Greeks that the validity of a given mathematical statement had to be demonstrated. Thales was reportedly a merchant, and may have encountered in his travels various formulas for the areas of planar figures and for the volumes of solid objects. Sometimes there would be different formulas for the same area or volume—say, for the volume of the frustum of a pyramid with a rectangular base; the frustum is the truncated pyramid that is cut off at some height h by a plane parallel to the base, as shown in the margin. The Babylonians had one formula for this object, and the Egyptians had another. (The Egyptians could have had a practical reason for developing accurate geometric formulas: they regularly had to measure their land, because the annual flooding of the river Nile obliterated almost all boundary markers in the flood plain.)

Now, given that there certainly could not be two correct formulas, Thales faced the problem of deciding, first, how to find the correct formula, and, second, how to convince others that this formula was valid. Certainly it was not a question for debate in the way that people could debate more subjective questions, such as which was the better of two fine works of art. The method that he evolved for discovering true statements about geometric figures constituted the beginnings of geometry, and the method that he used to convince his associates was probably the origin of the method of proof by deductive reasoning. (Incidentally, the formula developed by the Egyptians was the correct one.)

Thus, it is not surprising that Thales is said to be the creator of the first Greek geometry. The invention of geometry as an abstract mathematical theory supported by rigorous deductive proofs was certainly one of the turning points of scientific thinking. In particular, it led, as we shall see, to the creation of mathematical models for physical phenomena.

For instance, the Greeks had the concept of a curved line, which they defined as the trace of a point moving through space. Obviously the motion of a planet, if considered a point in the sky, would yield a fictitious curve in the firmament.

The simplest curves are *straight lines* and *circles*. The straight line is the shortest path joining two points in space. It is the trace of a fly (thought to be very, very small) that moves in the shortest way from one point to another. A circle is the set of all points in a plane that are at some fixed, equal distance from a center point. If you fix any point on a sphere, and rotate the sphere about a fixed axis, the point will describe a circle.

The beautifully symmetric circle does not, at first sight, seem to have a minimum property like the straight line. However, if we rotate a circle about one of its diameters, we generate a sphere. For any two points on the generating circle, the shortest path connecting these points on the sphere must be a subarc of this circle. (Another, very surprising optimum property of the circle also known to the Greeks is connected with "Queen Dido's problem," which we will consider later in this chapter.)

The scientists of antiquity used ideas about circles and spheres to create a mathematical model for the motion of the planets and the stars in the heavens. Pythagoras assumed the stars to be attached to a crystal sphere that revolved daily about an axis through the Earth. Similarly, the seven planets—Sun, Moon, Mercury, Mars, Jupiter, Venus, and Saturn—were each supposedly attached to a moving sphere of its own.

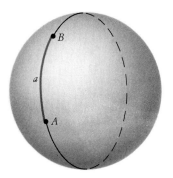

A *sphere* consists of all those points in space that are at some fixed, equal distance from a center point. The shortest connection between two points A and B on a sphere is an arc a of a great circle.

Pythagoras: a twelfth-century sculpture on
the Cathedral of Chartres.

This concept, later developed into a theory for the motion of the heavenly bodies, formed the basis of astronomy until the sixteenth century.
The Pythagorean model of the heavens was actually rather complex,
but we will mention only one other feature of it here.

The Pythagoreans believed that numbers were the key to understanding the order of the universe, and numbers meant to them whole
numbers (or integers, 1,2,3,4, . . .). Aristotle described their beliefs
in his *Metaphysics,* saying,

> the so-called Pythagoreans applied themselves to mathematics, and . . .
> came to believe that its principles are the principles of everything. And since
> *numbers* are by nature first among these principles, they fancied that they
> could detect in numbers, more than in fire and earth and water, many ana-
> logues of what is and what comes to be. . . . And since they saw further that
> the properties and ratios of the musical scales are based on numbers, that all
> other things are entirely modeled upon numbers, and that numbers are the
> ultimate things in the whole physical universe, they assumed the elements of
> numbers to be the elements of everything, and the whole universe to be a
> harmony or number.

In fact, Pythagoras had discovered a remarkable relation between numbers and musical sounds. For instance, if you pluck a taut string on a guitar, you produce a musical note. The pitch of the note produced depends on the length of the plucked string. Thus a player of a string instrument generates sounds of different pitches by changing the length of the vibrating string. The surprising observation of Pythagoras was that sounds produced by strings are harmonious if their lengths are in the ratio of whole numbers, say 1:2, 2:3, 3:4, or 5:8. In this way, harmony could be explained in terms of integers. To the Pythagoreans this discovery had a mystical significance. They concluded that all relations in nature could be expressed by integers and, accordingly, believed that the ratios of distances between celestial bodies would correspond to the ratios of lengths of harmonious chords. Then the heavenly spheres, as they revolved, produced harmonious sounds that only initiates could hear. This was the *music of the spheres* so often mentioned in literature.

The Pythagorean concept of heavenly harmony was perhaps the first abstract model that attempted to explain complex phenomena in nature by means of a simple and coherent mathematical theory. In fact, Pythagoras has turned out to be so important for the history of mathematics and physics that it is well worth our while to survey his life, legendary though its details may be.

It is reported that Pythagoras was born on the island of Samos, near Asia Minor. He visited Thales, who encouraged him to study in Egypt, the source of much of Thales' original knowledge. Pythagoras traveled in Egypt for many years, acquiring both mathematical and mystical knowledge. When he returned to Samos he founded a religious and philosophical society. For political reasons, Pythagoras eventually had to leave his homeland. He moved to Croton in southern Italy, where he had many supporters and followers.

The society that he founded had a strict set of beliefs and a fixed code of conduct. After a period of testing, the new initiates in the society were permitted to hear the Master's voice, but only from behind a curtain; several years later, when their souls were further purified by the Pythagorean lifestyle, they were permitted to actually see Pythagoras. The Pythagoreans believed that the soul could ascend through the spheres, to eventual union with God, by means of mathematics.

Many mathematical results are attributed to this society—for example, the *Pythagorean theorem*. It states that the sides of a right triangle are related by the formula $a^2 + b^2 = c^2$ in which c is the length of the longest side, and a and b are the lengths of the sides that meet

The Pythagorean theorem: in any right-angled triangle, $c^2 = a^2 + b^2$.

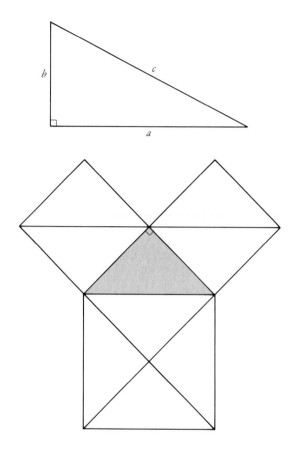

For an isosceles triangle, it is easy to see by inspection that the sum of the areas of the squares on the shorter sides equals the area of the square on the longer side.

perpendicularly. This theorem led the Pythagoreans to discover irrational numbers such as $\sqrt{2}$, the square root of two, when they tried to deal with a right triangle the short sides of which are each equal to one. The length of its longest side must satisfy the equation $c^2 = 1 + 1 = 2$, whence $c = \sqrt{2}$. From this we conclude that the number $\sqrt{2}$ must exist, because such a triangle exists. On the other hand, it is not difficult to prove that $\sqrt{2}$ cannot be written as a ratio of two integers.

The Pythagoreans were shocked to discover the existence of irrational numbers,* because these contradicted their belief that every-

---

* A number is called *irrational* if it cannot be expressed as the *ratio* of two integers, that is, if it is not a fraction like 2/3, 17/39, 14/63, ...

A proof that $\sqrt{2}$ is not a ratio of two integers.

To prove this, we will assume that the square root of 2 *is* a ratio of integers and show that the assumption leads to a contradiction. If $\sqrt{2} = P/Q$, in which P and Q are integers, then by dividing out all common factors, we could express $\sqrt{2}$ as p/q in which p and q are positive integers that now have no common integer factors. Suppose that we have $\sqrt{2} = p/q$ with such a pair p and q. If we square both sides of the equation to get $2 = p^2/q^2$ and then multiply both sides by q^2, we have $2q^2 = p^2$. Now let us make a table showing the possibilities for the final digits of $2q^2$ and p^2:

If a number ends in	0	1	2	3	4	5	6	7	8	9
then its square ends in	0	1	4	9	6	5	6	9	4	1
and twice its square ends in	0	2	8	8	2	0	2	8	8	2

Evidently, $2q^2$ must end in one of the digits of the third row, and p^2 must end in a digit of the second row. But the only digit that appears in both rows is 0; so the only way that $2q^2$ can be equal to p^2 is if both of them end in 0. This is possible only if p ends in 0 and q ends in either 0 or 5. In either case, both p and q must be divisible by 5. But this contradicts our assumption that we had divided out all the common factors in P and Q to obtain p and q. This contradiction shows that the original assumption, that $\sqrt{2} = P/Q$, cannot be correct. Therefore, the square root of 2 is not a ratio of two integers.

---

thing in the universe could be explained in terms of whole numbers and their ratios. At first they apparently tried to keep the unpleasant truth a secret. The discoverer, Hippasus of Metapontum, as one legend says, was even thrown overboard into the sea to drown after he had made this discovery during a voyage. Perhaps for the first time in scientific history, abstract thinking had led inexorably to a conclusion that totally shattered people's preconceptions.

The secrecy of the society and the mystical observances supposedly learned by Pythagoras in Egypt aroused much suspicion. About

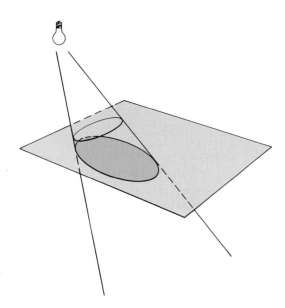

The ellipse as central projection of a circle.

A trochoid.

500 B.C., Pythagoras was forced to flee to Tarentum and then to Metapontum, where he was murdered. His followers continued to be active elsewhere until at least 400 B.C.

After the dissolution of the Pythagorean school, the study of geometry was continued by many other Greek schools. It is a basic principle of mathematics (as, it seems, of the human mind) to build more and more complicated structures out of simple ones. So from the straight line and the circle, which have such pleasing minimum properties, the Greeks were able to construct more complex curves. For example, let a circle roll on a straight line (in the way that the wheels of a train roll on rails) or on another circle. Consider the curve described by a fixed point on the periphery of the rolling circle. It is called a *cycloid* if the wheel rolls on a straight rail, an *epicycloid* if the wheel rolls on the outside of a circular rail, or a *hypocycloid* if it rolls on the inside of a circular rail.

Other curves, called *trochoids*, are created by a point attached to a wheel, but not necessarily to its rim, as the wheel rolls on a straight line or on the outside (*epitrochoid*) or inside (*hypotrochoid*) of another circle.

We can produce another kind of curve by projecting a circle along straight lines emanating from a fixed point, the center of projection (the light bulb in the illustration at the upper left), onto a fixed plane. This curve is an *ellipse;* it is one of the five *conic sections.* As the name implies, a conic section is produced when a plane intersects a cone of revolution. Such a cone can be obtained by rotating a line L through a point P about an axis A, as shown in the illustration on page 38. The result looks like two ice-cream cones with their tips touching. Point P is the *vertex* of the cone. Intersection of this cone by planes,

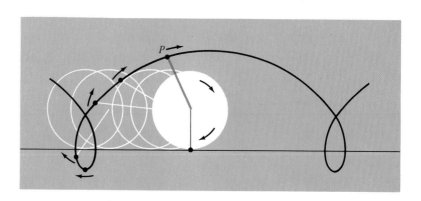

A cycloid (*A*), an epicycloid (*B*), and a hypocycloid (*C*).

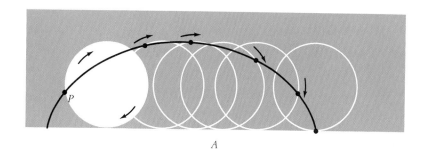

A

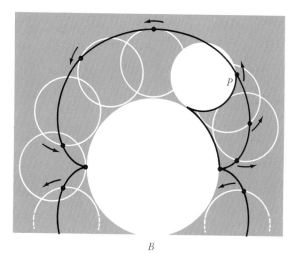

B

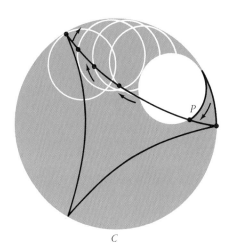

C

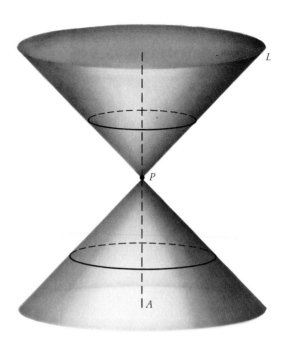

A cone of revolution.

each plane meeting the cone in more than one point (as shown in the illustration on the facing page), yields the five conic sections: the corresponding curves of intersection, in addition to the ellipse, are the *circle*, the *parabola*, the *hyperbola*, and the *straight line* (not shown in the illustration).

With the exception of the straight line, each conic section has either one or two focal points: the circle has one focus, its center, as does the parabola; the ellipse and the hyperbola have two foci, located on their major axes. Some of the remarkable properties of these points are described in the next section.

The main results on conic sections were found by Apollonius of Perga (262-190 B.C.). They are described in his eight books, *Conic Sections*, the first four of which were revisions of work done by Euclid, work that was subsequently lost forever.

The discovery of the conic sections is attributed to Menaechmus, a member of Plato's school of mathematics. This school flourished in the city state of Athens during the fourth century, just after the passing of the Golden Age of Pericles, the classic period of Greek art, architecture, and philosophy, when the Acropolis was built.

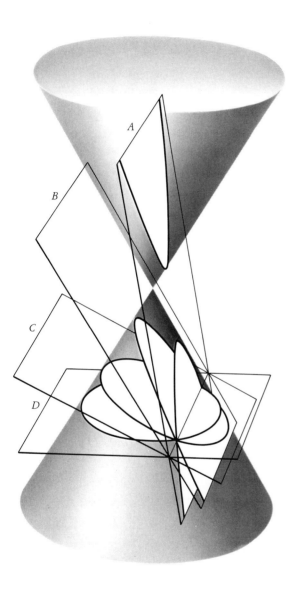

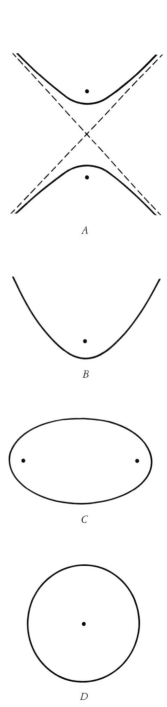

The conic sections: (A) hyperbola, (B) parabola, (C) ellipse, and (D) circle. Planar representations of these sections are shown at the right: (A) hyperbola, with its foci; (B) parabola, with its focus; (C) ellipse, with its foci; and (D) circle, with its center.

Plato, a student of Socrates, founded his school, the Academy, in a sacred area of Athens called Hekademeia (after a hero named Hekademos). All later academies obtained their name from this institution, which existed without interruption for about 1,000 years, until it was dissolved by the Emperor Justinian in A.D. 529. Plato's school was something like a small university, where the philosopher and his friends taught courses to students. Two of the greatest mathematicians of antiquity, Eudoxus of Cnidos (408–355 B.C.) and Theatetus (420–367 B.C.), were members of the Academy. Although Plato was not a mathematician, he appreciated this science so much that he required every student to devote ten years to the mathematical sciences, and five more to the true philosophy. The sign over the entrance to the Academy reputedly read, *"Let no one who is unacquainted with geometry enter here."*

It is reported that Plato suggested the following problem to his students: explain the motion of the heavenly bodies by combining various circular and spherical motions. Plato did not particularly appreciate astronomy as a practical science, useful for farmers and seamen alike. In his opinion, it deserved attention only as a playground for the geometer, to whom it was a source of interesting problems.

What problem did the motions of the planets pose? From the Earth, these motions appear to be quite complicated. The motion of the Sun and the Moon can be roughly described as circular with constant speed, but the deviations from the circular orbit were troublesome to the Greeks, and they felt challenged to find some explanations for those irregularities. The observed orbits of the planets are even more complicated, because, as the planets go through one revolution, they reverse direction for a time, then reverse again to go forward, all with changing speed. The Greeks sought to understand this seemingly wild motion by a geometric model.

Eudoxus took up this problem, and proposed an elegant and purely geometric theory of the celestial motions, which, however, had the serious shortcoming that it could not explain much of the empirical data. Thus, in the third century B.C., Apollonius of Perga suggested that the celestial orbits should be explained by means of combinations of circular motions, as in the construction of the epicycloid. This idea was to become the most important astronomical theory of the next two thousand years. It was worked out in detail by Hipparchus, the greatest astronomer of antiquity, in the second century B.C. His work is known to us through the celebrated *Mathematical Collection*, written by the Greek astronomer Ptolemy of Alexandria in the second century A.D., and called *al-Magest*, "the greatest," by Arabic-speaking astron-

The apparent motion of the planets. The photograph shows the movements of Mercury, Venus, Mars, Jupiter, and Saturn. The diagram shows the paths traced by the planets as seen from the Earth, which the Ptolemaic theory tried to explain.

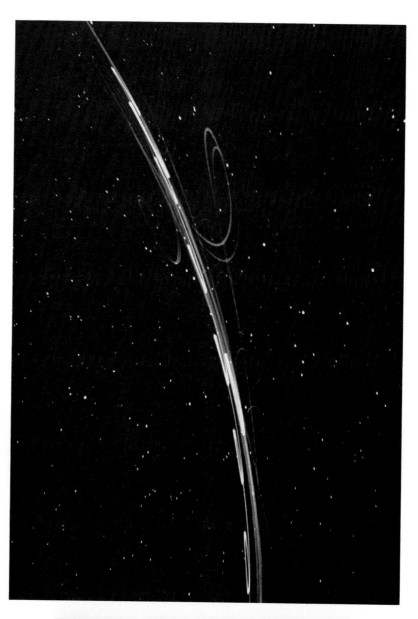

Galileo Galilei (1564–1642).

omers of the Middle Ages. This book completed the *geocentric system* of astronomy, which later was known as the *Ptolemaic system*. The theory of Ptolemy became so completely accepted that, in the Middle Ages, it was thought to have been handed directly to man by God.

It is not surprising that the Greek astronomers placed the Earth and not the Sun at the center of our universe, because we see the Sun rise every morning and sink below the horizon every evening. Still, we may wonder why the Greeks did not at least test the *heliocentric system*, which places the Sun at the center of the universe. In fact, Aristarchus of Samos, had conceived such a system in the third century B.C. He taught that the Earth and the other planets move in circular orbits around a fixed Sun. His hypotheses were not accepted for several reasons: the Greeks could not explain why objects would be able to stay on a moving Earth, why people did not sense that the Earth was moving, and why the clouds did not lag behind a moving Earth. These arguments were to be used against the heliocentric theory almost two thousand years later, when it was again proposed by the astronomer Nicolaus Copernicus.

Copernicus, born in 1473, studied at the University of Cracow but eventually went to Italy to visit Bologna, then a scientific center of Europe. There he learned how to make astronomical observations, a pastime which was to occupy him for the rest of his life. The upshot of his investigations was a truly remarkable book entitled *De Revolutionibus Orbium Coelestium* (*On the Revolutions of the Heavenly Orbits.*). There he introduced his heliocentric theory of the universe that was to bring about the "Copernican revolution" in science. However, he was cautious enough to delay publication of his ideas until he lay near death in 1543. Indeed, *De Revolutionibus* eventually was placed on the Papal index of forbidden books (in 1616).

Galileo Galilei took neither this, nor the burning at the stake of the astronomer Giordano Bruno by the Inquisition in 1600, as seriously as he should have. Ecclesiastical opposition to the ideas of Copernicus became enormous, because these ideas questioned a theory supported by the church authorities. In 1632, Galileo published his *Dialogue Concerning the Two Chief World Systems* debating the pros and cons of the heliocentric theory. This brought him into confrontation with the church and led to his trial, condemnation, recantation, and house arrest at the age of seventy.

As early as 1602, Galileo had discovered that heavy stones fall to the ground as quickly as do light ones. Thus he was led to the mechanical law that all falling bodies accelerate toward the Earth at the same rate, provided that the resistance of the air could be ignored. His cele-

Johannes Kepler (1571–1630).

brated formula $s = 16t^2$ states that a falling body has traveled the distance s (measured in feet) after a fall of t seconds. He used this discovery to solve an old problem of motion, the problem of finding the trajectory of a ball thrown into the air. Galileo stated and proved that such a ball will travel along a path shaped like a parabola, again disregarding the resistance of the air. This was probably the first time in the history of science that a conic section (other than a circle or straight line) had been used to describe a physical phenomenon.

Yet another scientific revolution was still to come. The German astronomer Johannes Kepler deprived the circle of its right to be the only adequate orbit for a heavenly body! After his studies in Tübingen, Kepler became a professor of mathematics and morals at Graz. In 1600 he came to Prague as an assistant to the famous Danish astronomer Tycho de Brahe, who had collected an enormous amount of new astronomical data that far surpassed that available to the ancient Greeks. After Brahe's death in 1601, Kepler succeeded him as "Imperial Mathematician" to Emperor Rudolf II, who had his residence in Prague. By working with Brahe's observations, Kepler was forced to the conclusion that the planets do not move in circular orbits with the Sun at the center, but in elliptical ones with the Sun at one of the foci. For the first time the ellipse entered astronomy, the very ellipse that had been studied as a purely mathematical object by Apollonius 2,000 years earlier.

The law of the elliptic orbits was only the first of three fundamental laws of planetary motion discovered by Kepler. This great astronomer had been convinced of the mathematical design of the universe but he always checked his theories against observed facts. Although his search for mathematical harmony led him to amazing flights of scientific fantasy, he eventually arrived at his celebrated third law. It states that the square of the time T that a planetary body requires to complete one orbit is proportional to the cube of the great axis a of its elliptical orbit. In mathematical terms, there is some number K, independent of the planet, such that $T^2 = K \cdot a^3$.

Kepler's second law states that if a planet moves from a point A to some point B in a certain amount of time, and moves from A' to B' in the same amount of time, the area of the sectors SAB and $SA'B'$ must be equal. In other words, "equal areas are swept out in equal times." This explains why planets or comets speed up as they near the Sun. For example, Halley's comet needs 75 years to complete one full orbit; yet it whips around the Sun in only a few days.

The discovery of these beautiful laws, which may be counted among the greatest achievements of the human mind, led Kepler to write in his *Harmony of the World* (1619):

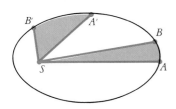

Kepler's second law.

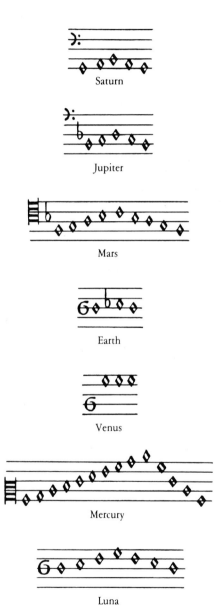

Saturn

Jupiter

Mars

Earth

Venus

Mercury

Luna

The Pythagoreans believed that the heavenly spheres, as they revolved, produced harmonious sounds. Reproduced here is the music of the planets as imagined by Kepler.

The wisdom of the Lord is infinite; so also are His glory and His power. Ye heavens, sing His praises! Sun, Moon, and planets, glorify Him in your ineffable language! Celestial harmonies, all ye who comprehend His marvelous works, praise Him. And thou, my soul, praise thy Creator! It is by Him and in Him that all exists. That which we know best is comprised in Him as well as in our vain science. To Him be praise, honor, and glory throughout eternity.

Thus what began with the spheres of Pythagoras and of Eudoxus, and with the circles of Apollonius, Ptolemy, and Copernicus, proceeded to the parabolas of Galileo and ended with the ellipses of Kepler. Isaac Newton based his enormously successful theory of gravitation on Kepler's and Galileo's results. From that theory, Euler derived an *optimum principle* describing the motions of the planets about the Sun, and his work was further developed by Lagrange, Hamilton, and Jacobi. Their work led to *variational principles,* on which all of classical mechanics could be built. The story leads on to atomic physics, quantum mechanics, and general relativity.

The Problem of Queen Dido

A celebrated maximum property of the circle already known in antiquity is connected with a story about Queen Dido of Carthage, which was told by the Roman poet Vergil (a contemporary of the Emperor Augustus) in his famous epic *Aeneid*.

Dido was a Phoenician princess from the city of Tyre (now part of Lebanon). She fled by ship from Tyre when King Pygmalion, her ruthless brother, murdered her husband to usurp her possessions. When Dido arrived in Africa about 900 B.C. at the place that later became Carthage, she tried to buy land from the local ruler, King Jarbas of Numidia, so that she and her people could settle and establish a new homeland for themselves. It could be that Dido was thrifty, or that Jarbas did not want any new settlements in his country: they concluded the bargain under the condition that the queen would obtain only as much land as she could enclose by the skin of an ox.

Dido made the most of the situation. First, she interpreted the word "enclose" as broadly as possible. Supposedly she had her people cut the hide in thin strips and tie them together to form a closed cord of great length. This length might have been between 1,000 and 2,000 yards if we assume that the width of the strips was as small as 1/10 inch.

Second, she spread the string on the ground in such a way that it enclosed the largest possible area. By assuming the ground to have been completely flat, we can imagine that Dido had to solve the following mathematical problem: "Among all possible closed curves of a given length, find those for which the area of the enclosed inner region is maximal." We may very well suppose that Dido found the correct solution, which is a circle whose circumference is of the prescribed length, and thus acquired an area between 25 and 60 acres. If the two ends of her string had been fixed at two points of a supposedly straight part of the beach of the Mediterranean sea, she would have obtained even more land, by spreading the cord in the form of a semi-circle; this is, in fact, what the story says she did. If you look at the maps of medieval European walled cities, you will find that their inhabitants usually came to the same conclusions as Dido.

Medieval map of Cologne.

Sailing around an island.

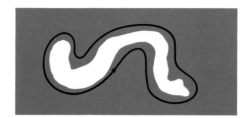

The Greeks were well aware of this mathematical task,* called the "isoperimetric problem" (*isos* = equal, *perimetron* = circumference), and they had obvious practical reasons for treating this problem. For example, can the size of an island be guessed from the time that it takes to sail around it? As the illustrations above show, clearly one could make terrible mistakes.

Clever people knew that a piece of land having a small periphery might be larger in area than some other piece that has a larger circumference. Thus they could cheat less-intelligent owners when exchanging their land, provided that the size of a field was measured by the time it took to walk around it. Such situations were described by Proclus about A.D. 450 in his commentary to Euclid's first book. We will return to the isoperimetric problem later to see that it has been one of the most stimulating and influential problems in the history of mathematics.

Incidentally, Vergil's *Aeneid* is the story of Aeneas of Troy, who, after the fall of his city to King Agamemnon, escaped by ship with some of his followers. He then traveled from Asia Minor through the Mediterranean sea, finally landing in Italy, where he founded the city of Rome. In his travels, he stopped at Carthage, where he met Dido. She fell in love with Aeneas and wanted to marry him. But Jupiter intervened and ordered Aeneas to leave Dido, who then, in desperation, killed herself. For this reason, Dante, in his *Divine Comedy*, condemned her to the second circle of hell. Henry Purcell, in the days of England's rise to empire, retold this story in his opera *Dido and Aeneas*.

---

* The first proof of the isoperimetric property of the circle appears in the commentary of Theon to Ptolemy's *Almagest* and in the collected works of Pappus. The author of the proof is Zenodoros, who must have lived sometime between Archimedes (died 212 B.C..) and Pappus (about A.D. 340), since he quotes Archimedes and is cited by Pappus. However, Zenodoros' proof still contained a gap that was not closed until the second half of the nineteenth century, when the German mathematician Weierstrass provided a complete proof in his lectures at the University of Berlin.

Aeneas and Dido: from Codex Vergilii
Romanus 3867 (probably from the seventh
century A.D.).

The Principle of the Reflection of Light, and the Burning Mirrors of Archimedes

The first optimum principle in physics explained the reflection of light by a curved mirror.

From the time of Pythagoras, the Greeks had studied light rays. As early as 490 B.C. Empedocles of Agrigentum (in Sicily) stated that light travels through space with finite speed. This truly remarkable insight was only verified in 1676 by the Danish astronomer and mathematician Ole Rømer (1644–1710).

Most of what was known about light in Greek times appears in a work attributed to Euclid (about 330–270 B.C.). He lived in the city of Alexandria, which was founded in 331 B.C. by the emperor Alexander (unfortunately called the Great) at the mouth of the river Nile. Under the dynasty of the Ptolemies it became the scientific center of the world, a position that it maintained for 500 years. After the fall of the city-state of Athens in 338 B.C., Alexandria became the focal point of Greek culture. In this metropolis, knowledge was collected from and transmitted to the whole ancient world. About 285 B.C., the Museum (or *Museion,* "temple of the Muses") was founded. This was a cultural institution where scholars could work and study. At its peak, the celebrated library of the Museum supposedly contained about 750,000 manuscripts. In Alexandria, Euclid wrote his *Elements* (of mathematics), which became one of the most widespread books in the Western world (about 1,700 editions are known to exist). Actually, the *Elements* consists of thirteen books, in which Euclid collected most of the mathematical knowledge of his age, transformed into a lucid, logically developed masterpiece. The *Elements* is primarily a work on geometry; however, it also contains theorems on number theory and results on areas and volumes. King Ptolemy Soter of Alexandria is said to have asked Euclid if geometry could not be learned by an easier way than by reading the *Elements.* The mathematician's well-known answer was: *"There is no royal road to geometry."*

In addition to the *Elements,* other of Euclid's writings that have been handed down to us include the *Optics* and the *Catoptrica** ("theory of mirrors"). These books remained until the seventeenth century as basic to geometric optics as the *Elements* was to mathematics.

---

* The *Catoptrica* is probably not a genuine work of Euclid, but was attributed to him by later writers. Hence it is not known who discovered the law of reflection; yet it seems certain that it was known to Archimedes.

Euclid stated in his *Optics* that *"light travels through space along straight lines."* He then used this and other results to discuss the nature of vision. In the *Catoptrica*, he gave the fundamental *law of reflection*, which states the following two rules for a light ray striking a mirror and being reflected from that mirror:

> RULE 1. The plane of incidence of the ray coincides with its plane of reflection.
>
> RULE 2. The angle of incidence of the ray equals its angle of reflection.

Assume that the incident ray hits the mirror at point P, and consider the perpendicular L to the mirror at this point. Then the plane that contains the incident ray and the perpendicular is called the *plane of incidence*, whereas the *plane of reflection* is the plane that contains the reflected ray and the perpendicular. Consider the acute angle between the incident ray and the perpendicular. Its complement to a right angle is called the *angle of incidence*. Correspondingly, the complement of the acute angle between the reflected ray and the perpendicular to a 90° angle is the *angle of reflection*.

Then, by Rule 1, *the incident and reflected rays lie in the same plane perpendicular to the mirror.* This perpendicular plane intersects the mirror in a planar curve C, which for a flat mirror is a straight line. The construction of the reflected ray is now a planar problem that can be solved solely in the plane containing the curve C. By Rule 2 the angles of incidence and reflection in this plane must be equal. Thus we are led to the *reflection of light rays at planar curves*.

About 400 years after Euclid, the Alexandrian scientist Heron (about A.D. 100) saw a more fundamental law behind the law of reflection. He stated that this law follows from the principle that *light must always take the shortest path*. To illustrate this, let us consider the reflection from a flat mirror. This problem was seen to be equivalent to the reflection of a ray at a straight line. Hence, let us suppose that on one side of a curve we have two points P and Q, and that we want to travel from P, touch the curve, and then go on to Q. The question then is, what is the shortest path that we can find to accomplish this objective.

The same mathematical problem can be posed as a somewhat different "real world" problem. Suppose that a cowboy out on the prairie wishes at dusk to return to the ranch; yet his horse is very thirsty. The ranch is on the same side of a straight river as the rider. What is the shortest path that the rider can take back home and first water his horse at the river? Heron's answer is that he should travel

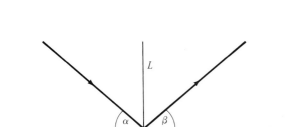

The angle of incidence α equals the angle of reflection β.

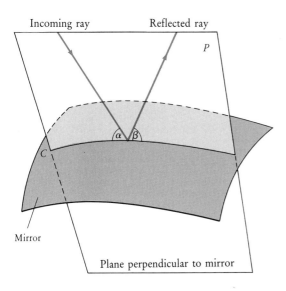

The law of reflection for a curved mirror: $\alpha = \beta$.

What is the shortest path from P to Q via M?
That is, what is the shortest path for a cowboy who wants, on his way home, to water
his horse?

Solution of the horse-watering problem.

along a straight line from point P to a point R at the river and then by
a straight line from R to Q, where R is chosen so that the angle of
incidence equals the angle of reflection. A short proof of Heron's theorem is given in the legend for the figure on page 51.

The question "What is the shortest path?" is indeed a very natural one. We have all at one time or another been in a great hurry to
reach some place, and have wondered how to get there in the shortest
possible way. The preceding problem can be generalized in many possible ways; let us look at a few of them. Consider, for example, two
points P and Q between two lines L and M. We can ask what the
shortest path from P to Q is that first touches line L, then touches
line M, and finally goes to Q. The answer is a broken line that satisfies
the law of reflection both at L and at M.

In our first examples we have considered reflections at straight
lines, which correspond to reflection by flat mirrors. The Greeks also
investigated reflections by curved mirrors or at curved lines, including
conic sections.

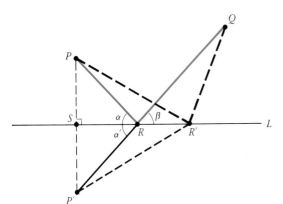

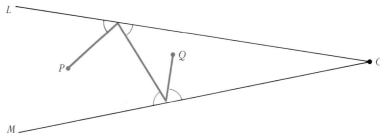

The shortest path between two points P and Q that first touches line L and then line M.

A PROOF OF HERON'S THEOREM

Because a straight line is the shortest connection between two points, we may assume that the shortest path consists of straight lines. Suppose that the shortest path touches line L at some point R. To find the point R, draw the perpendicular from P to L, with the foot on L at S. On this line mark off a distance from S below L equal to the distance $\overline{PS}$. This determines a point P'. Let R be the intersection point of L with the straight line drawn through P' and Q. Then draw the line from P to R. Note that the three angles α, α', and β at R are equal. Let R' be any other point on L. From the fact that the sum of two sides of a triangle is greater than the third, it follows that PRQ is the shortest possible path joining P and Q which touches L.

Let us begin with an *ellipse*. As we have already seen, the Greeks knew that every ellipse has two foci, say, P and Q. These foci have a remarkable property:

> For all points R on the ellipse, the sum $\overline{PR} + \overline{QR}$ of the distances of R to P and Q has the same value, say, the value d. Moreover, for any point R in the plane, the value of the sum $\overline{PR} + \overline{QR}$ is smaller than d, larger than d, or equal to d if R lies inside, outside, or on the ellipse, respectively.

Let us now draw the tangent line to the ellipse at some point R as shown in the illustration below. Then the property of the ellipse just stated implies that the broken path from P to R and then on to Q must be the shortest possible path from P to Q by way of the tangent line. Using Heron's result that the minimum-path property implies the law of reflection, we find that the angle of incidence must equal the angle of reflection. This means that the light rays emanating from one focus will be reflected by the ellipse in such a way that all of them pass

Reflection of light within an ellipse.

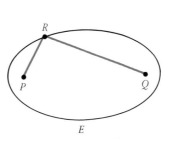

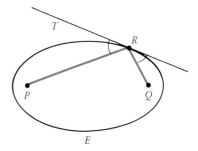

Reflection by a parabola: (*A*) a parabola with focus *P; (B)* all parallel rays are reflected through the parabola's focus.

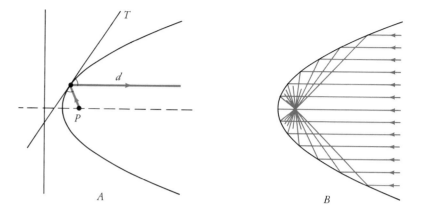

through the other focus. If we now generate an elliptical mirror by revolving the ellipse about its major axis (which is the straight line through its foci), we obtain a mirror with the following frightening property: if we place an intense light source, such as the Sun, at one of the foci, then its rays will all be collected at the other focus, burning everything found there.

A parabola has similar burning properties. In a way, a parabola can be considered an ellipse in which one of its foci has been moved to infinity. Therefore, all the light rays that emanate from the focus form a bundle of parallel rays, after they have been reflected by the parabola. Imagine the reverse situation—namely, many light rays coming in from a great distance away, as from the Sun. These rays would effectively be parallel to one another; so the parabola would reflect them all, causing them to meet at one point, at the focus of the parabola. Let us rotate the flat parabola about its axis to form a three-dimensional parabolic mirror. Such a mirror would collect all rays parallel to its axis at the focal point. Anything at this focus would be quickly incinerated. For this reason, the Sun could be used as a terrible weapon.*

In 216 B.C. the city of Syracuse in Sicily, which was part of Greek civilization, had allied itself with the city of Carthage in its

---

* In general, one cannot focus a mirror on an object to be burned *and,* at the same time, receive the Sun's rays parallel to the axis. Instead the solar rays and the axis of the parabolic mirror will form an angle, and after reflection, the rays will not focus in a single point, but will form a surface called a *caustic* or *burning surface.* This is a very complicated geometric object, but, in a first approximation, it often has a cusp point, and it turns out that most of the rays pass through a minute ball around this cusp. Hence there is a strong concentration of rays near the cusp point, and consequently the burning effect can still be achieved.

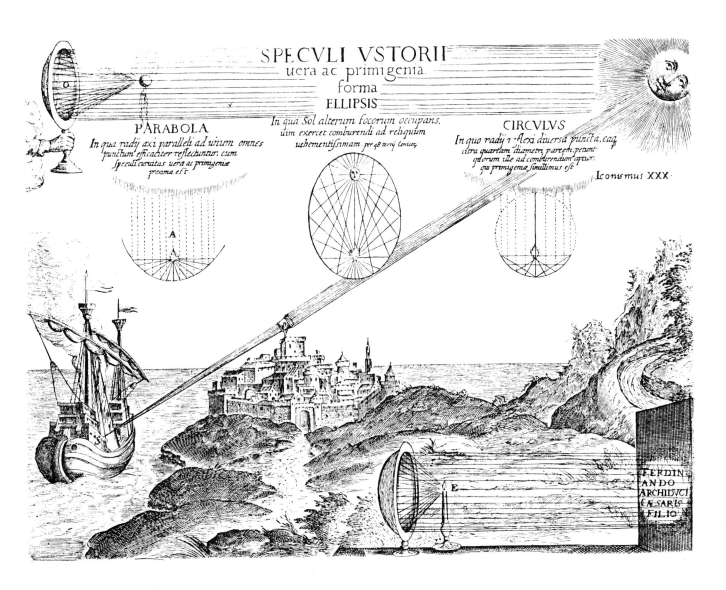

SPECVLI VSTORII
uera ac primigenia
forma
ELLIPSIS

PARABOLA

In qua radij axi paralleli ad unum omnes
punctum efficaciter reflectuntur, cum
speculi curuitas uera ac primigenia
proxima est.

In qua Sol alterum focorum occupans,
uim exercet comburendi ad reliquum
uehementissimam per 48 tertij Conicor.

CIRCVLVS

In quo radij reflexi diuersa puncta, eaq́;
citra quartam diametri partem petunt
qd'orum ille ad comburendum aptior,
qui primigenia simillimus est.

Iconismus XXX.

FERDIN
ANDO
ARCHIDVCI
CÆSARIS
FILIO

Seventeenth-century representation of the
burning mirrors.

battle against Rome during the second of the three Punic wars. As a
result of this coalition, in 214 B.C. the Romans laid siege to Syracuse.
Legend tells us that the "burning mirrors" of Archimedes enabled the
citizens of this ancient city to use the bright Sicilian summer sun to
incinerate the Roman fleet. What were these mirrors?

Archimedes (287–212 B.C.), the greatest mathematician of antiquity, spent most of his life in his native town of Syracuse. It is said that

Archimedes' theorem: the ratios of the volumes of a cone, half-ball, and cylinder, all of the same height and radius, are 1:2:3.

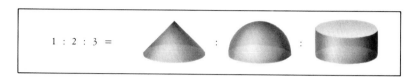

he completed his studies at Alexandria's Museum, but we know for certain only that he visited Egypt on at least one occasion.

The scientific fame of Archimedes is based mainly on his numerous mathematical discoveries. For instance, he found an excellent approximation for the value of π, the area enclosed by a circle of radius 1. He was able to show that π must be a number between $3\frac{1}{7}$ and $3\frac{10}{71}$. Moreover, he calculated many difficult volumes of bodies and areas of surfaces, such as the volume of a ball of radius r ($4\pi r^3/3$) and its surface area ($4\pi r^2$). In fact he proved that the volumes of a cone, of a half-ball, and of a cylinder, all of the same radius and height, are in the ratio 1:2:3, a theorem of which he was very proud. These mathematical results by Archimedes were truly astounding accomplishments for their time.

Archimedes, in addition to having been an extraordinarily gifted mathematician, was a mechanical genius as much admired by his contemporaries as by later writers. Among his celebrated inventions were the *Archimedean screw*, a machine for raising water, which was used in Egypt for the irrigation of fields and in Spain for pumping water out of mines, and the *Planetarium*, a set of spheres in which the motion of celestial bodies was imitated by a clever mechanism. Large specimens of such contrivances can nowadays be found in many of the great museums of science. Apparently they were as popular in antiquity as they are now. The writer Claudianus (about A.D. 400) described the amazement of Jupiter on seeing his work copied in a glass sphere by a mathematician from Syracuse, and Cicero reported that Marcellus, the conqueror of Syracuse in 212 B.C., took two planetaria as his only booty from the captured city.

Yet the greatest fame of Archimedes in antiquity resulted not from his peaceful inventions, but from his contributions to the defense of Syracuse against the Romans. When the Romans besieged the city in 214 B.C., they met an enemy who had been supplied by the 73-year-old mathematician with unexpected and powerful weapons. The approaching Roman legions were knocked down by a very effective artillery, which discharged long-range stone missiles, and by an enormous number of short-range projectiles. The ships of the Roman fleet were sunk by huge cranes, which either dropped stones on them or lifted their bows with an iron hand and then suddenly smashed them onto the water. Plutarch (in his *Life of Marcellus*) reported the commander Marcellus as saying to his army:

> Shall we not make an end of fighting against this geometric Briareus [a hundred-armed giant of Greek legend], who uses our ships to ladle water from the sea, who has ignominiously threshed and driven off the sambuca [the Roman assaulting ladder, used for the scaling of the walls of a besieged city], and who by the multitude of missiles that he hurls at us all at once outdoes the hundred-armed giants of mythology?

The Roman soldiers were terrified. Plutarch reported:

> If they only saw a rope or a piece of wood extending beyond the walls, they took flight, exclaiming that Archimedes had once again invented a new machine for their destruction.

But for the Roman soldiers, the worst was still to come: the incineration of their ships by the "burning mirrors" of Archimedes. Were such mirrors actually used? They were not described by contemporary historians, but appear only in stories written much later. They are mentioned for the first time in a book by Galen (A.D. 129–199), one of the two great physicians of antiquity besides Hippocrates. In 1200 the Byzantine historian Tsetses, unfortunately not a particularly trustworthy writer, gave the following account of what Archimedes supposedly had accomplished:

> When the Roman vessels were within bowshot range, Archimedes made a kind of hexagonal mirror, and small ones with 24 sides, which he placed at an appropriate distance and which he could move with the aid of hinges and metal wires. He arranged the hexagonal mirror so that it was bisected by the meridian of winter and summer, and the suns rays received by this mirror, after being reflected, kindled a great fire which reduced the Roman vessels to ashes, even though they moved out of bow's reach.

Such an array of reflecting plates could have created the same effect as a parabolic mirror. In the sixth century, the mathematician and architect Antheminus also suggested that Archimedes had used a hexagonal mirror. Many historians have dismissed this story as pure myth. The claims and doubts about Archimedes' brilliant accomplishment have stirred up a great deal of controversy for centuries. However, the feasibility of Archimedes' contrivance has been demonstrated

Death of Archimedes. Mosaic, probably from
the school of Raphael.

experimentally, in 1747 by the French naturalist Georges Buffon and
in 1973 by the Greek engineer Ioannis Sakkas.

The siege of Syracuse lasted two years, and the city only fell by
treason. In the aftermath of the assault, the old scientist was slain by a
Roman soldier, even though the commander Marcellus had asked his
men to spare Archimedes' life. As legend goes, Archimedes was sitting in front of his house studying some geometric figures drawn in the
sand. When a Roman soldier approached, Archimedes shouted out,
"Don't disturb my figures." The ruffian, feeling insulted, slew the
great man.

Marcellus, as some compensation, erected a tomb for Archimedes on which was depicted a sphere circumscribed by a cylinder, sym-
bolizing, according to Archimedes' wishes, his favorite theorem about
the volumes of the cone, cylinder, and sphere. When Cicero (106–43
B.C.) visited Sicily, he was able to locate the monument, overgrown
with underbrush and thorns.

Archimedes apparently considered his contributions to engineering to be of minor rank, unworthy of later remembrance. Plutarch
reported the following:

He did not deign to leave behind him any written work on such subjects; he regarded as sordid and ignoble the construction of instruments, and in general every art directed to use and profit, and he only strove after those things which, in their beauty and excellence, remain beyond all contact with the common needs of life.

If we think of all the horror caused by the scientific and engineering contrivances used in a multitude of wars, Archimedes' approach appears to be rather reasonable. The great English mathematician G. H. Hardy wrote in 1940:

> There is a real mathematics of the real mathematicians, and there is what I will call the "trivial" mathematics, for want of a better word. The trivial mathematics may be justified by arguments . . . , but there is no such defense for the real mathematics, which must be justified as art if it can be justified at all. There is nothing in the least paradoxical or unusual in this view, which is held commonly by mathematicians. . . . There is one comforting conclusion which is easy for a real mathematician. Real mathematics has no effects on war. No one has yet discovered any warlike purpose to be served by the theory of numbers or relativity, and it seems very unlikely that anyone will do so for many years. It is true that there are branches of applied mathematics, such as ballistics and aerodynamics, which have been developed deliberately for war and demand a quite elaborate technique: it is perhaps hard to call them "trivial," but none of them has any claim to rank as "real." They are indeed repulsively ugly and intolerably dull. . . . So a real mathematician has his conscience clear; there is nothing to be set against any value his work may have; mathematics is, as I said at Oxford, a harmless and innocent occupation. The trivial mathematics, on the other hand, has many applications in war. . . . And the general effect of these applications is plain: mathematics facilitates (if not so obviously as physics or chemistry) modern, scientific, "total" war.

Alas, there is no pure, innocent mathematics. Even number theory, the favorite of Hardy, is now a tool in the hands of the secret services.

3

Shortest and Quickest Connections

"Undoubtedly," said Wimsey, "but if you think that this identification is going to make life one grand, sweet song for you, you are mistaken . . . . Since we have devoted a great deal of time and thought to the case on the assumption that it was murder, it's a convenience to know that the assumption is correct."

(Lord Peter Wimsey, in Dorothy L. Sayers's *Have His Carcase*)

At one time or another, we have all considered a problem in the calculus of variations. When planning an automobile trip, we wonder which route is the shortest, or quickest, to our destination. The answers to these two questions are not necessarily the same: it might be quicker to choose a detour on a highway than to take a shorter connection by a small and crooked road that leads through a mountainous area.

Problems of this kind were of interest to the Romans, who connected Italy with the other provinces of their empire by an excellent system of roads. Good roads allowed rapid movements of the Roman legions to suppress any rebellion; yet a rebellion could therefore also very quickly reach Rome itself.

Leonhard Euler (1707–1783).

Gerardus Mercator (1512–1594).

Hermann Amandus Schwarz (1843–1921).

The question of shortest or quickest connections became especially important to the European powers during the fifteenth and sixteenth centuries, when they were searching for the best routes to the Far East and to the New World. Faster sailing routes promised greater profits. The well-known expeditions of Vasco da Gama and of Christopher Columbus must be seen mainly in economic terms.

No wonder that in this period the spherical shape of the Earth again became common knowledge. The early Greeks had imagined the Earth to be a flat disc, surrounded by the ocean and vaulted by the heavens. However, Pythagoras had taught that the Earth was spherical in shape, and Aristotle as well as Archimedes tried to give proofs of this fact. Eratosthenes (about 275–195 B.C.), principal of the Alexandrian library, even derived a fairly accurate value for the circumference of our planet, of about 37,000 kilometers. The spherical shape of the Earth was certainly common knowledge to the educated in ancient Greece; yet, in late Roman times, this geographical knowledge was rarely remembered. Most of the Church Fathers inferred from the Bible that the Earth must be a flat disc. Accordingly it was depicted as a wheel having Jerusalem as its center. However, Greek geography was never quite forgotten and, during the Renaissance, Greek writings were rediscovered, and science revived. In 1492, when Christopher Columbus discovered America, Martin Behaim constructed the first globe since antiquity. With the increase of trade and navigation, the preparation of accurate maps became a major scientific task. The cartographer Gerardus Mercator was one of the first to draw charts based on mathematical principles. (It was Gauss who only later understood the basic mathematical principles of map making. We will discuss some of his achievements later.)

The mathematical theory of shortest lines on surfaces, such as on the surface of the Earth, was founded in 1697 by the brothers Jacob and Johann Bernoulli. Before we look at this theory, we will consider some simpler questions that can be answered by reasoning taken solely from elementary geometry.

The first problem we will examine was posed and solved by Hermann Amandus Schwarz, a professor first at Göttingen and then at Berlin, and one of the most distinguished researchers on the calculus of variations in the nineteenth century. He often enjoyed writing on elementary subjects, and the following problem appears in one of his papers.

Given an acute triangle, that is, one in which all angles are less than 90°, find an inscribed triangle with the smallest possible perimeter.

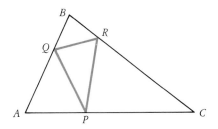

Inscribed triangle.

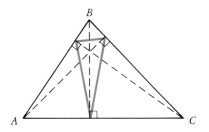

Altitude triangle.

Karl Weierstrass (1815–1897).

By *inscribed triangle* in a given triangle *ABC*, we mean a triangle such that each of its vertices *P,Q,R* touches a different side of *ABC*.*

The answer to the minimum question is not at all obvious. Schwarz discovered that the inscribed triangle of shortest perimeter is given by the *altitude triangle*. The vertices *P*, *Q*, *R* of the altitude triangle are obtained by dropping the perpendicular from each vertex *A*, *B*, *C* to its opposite side.

Let us see why this triangle is indeed the solution of Schwarz's problem. From Heron's principle, it follows that any solution must be a *light triangle*. What do we mean by this? If we think of the triangle *ABC* as a triangular room with mirrors as walls, such an inscribed triangle represents a closed path of travel for a ray of light in the room. Thus, at each vertex of this triangle, the adjacent angles are equal (see the lower illustration at the left). By elementary geometric reasoning, it follows that the *altitude triangle* is the only inscribed light triangle.

You might think that, by the preceding arguments, we have outlined a complete proof of Schwarz's theorem; yet we have not. We have proved only that, *if there is a solution of Schwarz's problem, it has to be the altitude triangle. But it is by no means clear that there is any solution.* This may look like hair splitting, but, in fact, it is absolutely necessary that we be meticulous with our proof. In order to convince you, we suggest that you put yourself in the position of Lord Peter Wimsey. Suppose that Wimsey has found the dead body of a man and that he has seventeen suspects. Moreover, he is completely sure that no one else could be the murderer. By collecting all the evidence and by checking the alibis, he then reduces the number of suspects one by one, and finally only one remains: the butler. Hence the butler is the murderer! But wait. Peter is very careful. By checking the evidence once more, he manages to prove beyond doubt that the dead man died by suicide; so there is no murderer. You see the point: it does not suffice to find a clear and uniquely determined suspect in your criminal case; you also must prove that it is a case of murder.

The same principle applies to our mathematical problem. The altitude triangle is our only candidate for a solution of Schwarz's problem, but we also have to prove that a solution exists.

You might feel embarrassed if you fell into the trap of thinking that we have a complete proof, but you are in good company, for the greatest mathematicians, including Riemann, made this kind of mistake. Only Karl Weierstrass, professor at the University of Berlin,

---

*We could also ask for the inscribed triangle of largest perimeter. Yet the solution to this problem is completely obvious. It is the original triangle *ABC* itself.

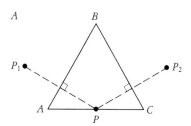

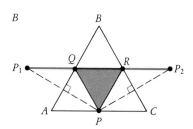

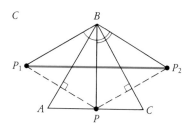

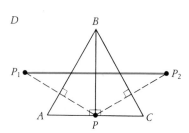

An elementary proof of the existence of a solution to Schwarz's problem.
A. The reflection of a point, P, across two
sides of a triangle.
B. An arbitrary inscribed triangle with one
vertex at P.
C. Is there a point P on edge AC for which
the distance P_1P_2 of its mirror image is
minimal?
D. Yes, it is the foot of the altitude from B.

convinced his contemporaries in 1869 by a striking example that, in
order to solve a minimum problem, you must not only track down all
the possible candidates for its solution, but also prove that the problem
possesses at least one solution.

Here is another example, in case our Lord Peter Wimsey story
has not erased all your doubts.

We know that 1 is the smallest number among all positive integers 1, 2, 3, 4, 5, etc. Assuming that there is a largest integer, we are
now going to "prove" that 1 is the largest integer as well. To this end,
take any integer n *different from* 1. Then n is smaller than n^2, which is
also an integer. Thus n cannot be the largest integer, and therefore 1,
being the only remaining possibility, must be the largest of all numbers
1, 2, 3, ...

The obvious mistake in this argument is that we assumed the
existence of a largest integer.

After the criticism of Weierstrass, mathematicians worked out a
kind of reasoning, known as *the direct method in the calculus of variations,* that often enables them to prove the existence of a solution to a
given minimum or maximum problem. For Schwarz's problem it is,
fortunately, fairly easy to prove the existence of a solution by elementary geometric arguments.

To this end, we choose an arbitrary point P on edge AC, as
shown at the left, and reflect it at edges AB and BC. Let P_1 and P_2 be
the corresponding mirror images of P. Next, we pick two other points,
Q and R, on sides AB and BC, respectively, and consider the inscribed
triangle PQR. Its perimeter is equal to the total length L of the line
segments P_1QRP_2; that is,

$$L = \overline{P_1Q} + \overline{QR} + \overline{RP_2}.$$

If we fix P on AC, this length L will be smallest if both Q and R lie on
the straight line through P_1 and P_2; so L will be equal to $\overline{P_1P_2}$, the
distance between the points P_1 and P_2.

Thus Schwarz's problem is reduced to the question of whether
there exists a position of point P on edge AC for which the distance
$\overline{P_1P_2}$ is minimal. We claim that this distance is least when P is the foot
of the perpendicular from B to side AC. First, note that triangle P_1BP_2
is isosceles, because B is at the same distance from the three points
P, P_1, P_2; that is, $\overline{P_1B} = \overline{PB} = \overline{P_2B}$. Moreover, the angle of this isosceles
triangle at B turns out (as you can see from part C of the figure at the
left) to be independent of the position of P (it is twice the angle of the
triangle ABC at B). An isosceles triangle with a fixed angle subtended
by the two equal sides will have the smallest possible base (in this case

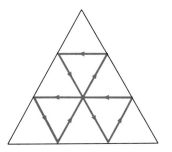

A closed path of light need not be minimal.

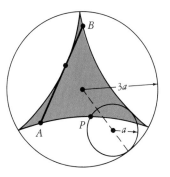

Hypocycloid and needle.

Jacob Steiner (1796–1863).

$\overline{P_1P_2}$) when the length of its two equal sides is minimal, and thus when $\overline{PB}$ is minimal. Because the shortest distance from a point to a line is the perpendicular to that line, it follows that PB is minimal if P coincides with the foot of the perpendicular from B to AC.

Hence we have proved that Schwarz's problem possesses a solution and that this solution is furnished by triangle PQR (see part B) in which P is the foot of the altitude from B to AC (see part D) and Q and R are intersection points of line P_1P_2 with edges AB and BC, respectively. Because the altitude triangle was the only one that could be a solution, we may infer that *the altitude triangle is the one and only solution of Schwarz's problem,* as we had claimed.

We conclude our remarks on Schwarz's problem with the observation that, besides the light triangle, there are other possible closed paths of light, as indicated in the upper illustration at the left. All follow the law of reflection. Schwarz's triangle is the only closed path of light that consists of only three straight segments.

As we have seen, it is essential to prove that a solution to a given mathematical problem actually exists. Yet you might think that every "reasonable" mathematical question must have a solution. Here is an example that proves otherwise.

In 1917 the Japanese mathematician Kakeya proposed the following problem:

Find a figure of least area in which a segment of length 1 can be turned through 360° by a continuous movement.

(You might think of a very thin needle that is to be turned around in a flat container.)

The "feeling" was that Kakeya's problem should have a solution. For a time, it was believed that a hypocycloid of area $\pi/8$ was the desired figure (see the middle illustration at the left). However, in 1927, Besicovitch published the following surprising result:

There are figures of arbitrarily small area in which it is possible to turn a segment of length 1 through 360° by a continuous movement, remaining always in the figure.

This implies that Kakeya's problem has no solution—a complete surprise to anyone who has not seen this question before.

Let us consider another beautiful example of a minimum problem that can be solved by elementary geometry combined with a minimum principle. It was devised by Jakob Steiner, a professor at the University of Berlin.

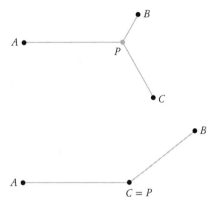

A path of minimal length connecting three points.

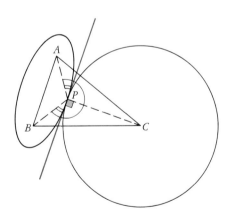

The solution to Steiner's problem.

The generalized Steiner problem.

Three cities A, B, and C are to be connected by a system of roads. Let us assume that there are no obstructions, so that we are free to build the roads as we please, and that the region around the cities is flat. The problem is to find the system of least possible total length. To paraphrase this mathematically, we are given three points A, B, and C in a plane and are required to find a point P, and paths that join P to A, B, and C, such that the total length of the paths is a minimum. Because a straight line is the shortest path between two points, we can further assume that these lines are straight.

The nature of the solution depends on how the points are situated. If all the angles of triangle ABC are less than 120°, then P is the point within this triangle at which the angles APC, CPB, and BPA are equal, and hence each is equal to 120° (see the upper illustration at the left). However, if one of the angles (say, the angle at C) in the triangle ABC is greater than 120°, then the solution point P must be point C.

Again, some elementary geometry and an application of Heron's law of reflection will lead us to the only candidate for a solution.

Suppose that the center point P of some solution to Steiner's problem does not coincide with one of the vertices A, B, or C. Then let us consider a circle centered at C and an ellipse with A and B as its foci, constructed so that both the circle and the ellipse pass through P (see the drawing at the left). By the minimum property of point P, the circle and the ellipse then have a common tangent at P, and P is the only point that they have in common. The reflection property of the ellipse (described on pp. 51–52) implies that angles APC and BPC are equal. If we centered the circle at B instead and used A and C as the foci of the ellipse, we would see that angles BPC and BPA must be equal. Because the sum of these three equal angles at P is 360°, each angle is 120°. It follows from elementary geometry that P lies within the triangle ABC and is uniquely determined, provided its existence is known. As with Schwarz's problem, an existence proof can be given.

It is of great interest to us that if the solution point P is not a vertex, then equal angles of 120° must be formed by the connecting lines about P. Later, when we treat soap films, soap bubbles, and cracks in certain materials, the 120° angle will repeatedly occur. More-

Two different solutions to the same generalized Steiner problem with four end points.

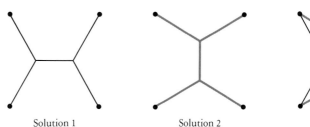

Solution 1   Solution 2   Both solutions

over, we shall see that soap films can be used to obtain a physical
solution to Steiner's problem.

There is a much more general version of Steiner's problem, in
which many points in a plane must be connected by a system of lines of
smallest total length. Such a problem must be solved in order to design
a highway network that is to connect three or more cities and is to be
built at the least possible cost.

A solution of such a *generalized Steiner problem* will be in some
sense a combination of the two possibilities shown above. Some possible configurations of solutions are shown at the bottom of the facing
page. Notice that a solution to Steiner's general problem is not always
unique. For example, two possible networks of equal minimal total
lengths, joining the four corners of a square, are shown above.

Another type of minimum problem is to find the shortest path
between a point and a curve, or the shortest path between two curves.
By the Pythagorean theorem, the shortest connection from a point P
to a straight line L can be found by dropping the *perpendicular* onto L.
The perpendicular is the straight line through P that intersects L in a
right angle at some point P^*.

From this fact you can deduce that the shortest connection from
a point P to a closed convex curve C (where P is supposed to be inside
C) will meet this curve in an angle of 90° at some point P^*. Just draw
the tangent line L to C at P^*; the segment $\overline{PP^*}$ will then yield the
shortest distance from P to L, and so each of the angles at P^* enclosed
by L and PP^* will be a right angle.

The shortest path from a point to a line.

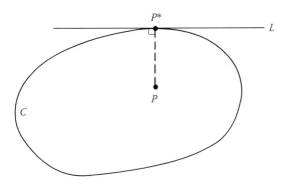

The shortest path from a point to a closed,
convex curve.

The shortest path from a point to a
smooth curve.

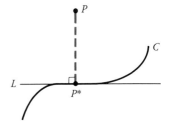

Finally, we note that even for an arbitrary smooth curve C, the shortest connection between some point P and the curve will meet C in a right angle; but a correct proof of this fact needs some infinitesimal calculus.

Similarly, the shortest path joining two curves C_1 and C_2 meets both of them in a right angle. Recall what we noticed in the Prologue: soap films, when free to move on other surfaces, always meet them perpendicularly, and cracks in certain materials intersect each other at angles of 90°.

In the following discussion, we will see perpendicularity play an important role in another, 300-year-old problem of shortest connection that we stated at the beginning of this chapter. It is the problem of finding the shortest path between two points on a curved surface. This has been, and remains, one of the fundamental problems in geometry.

The shortest path joining two smooth curves C_1 and C_2 meets both of them at a right angle.

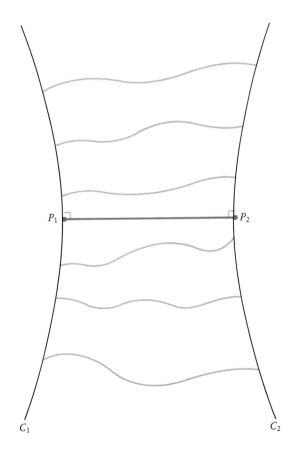

As we saw, the Greeks knew that the shortest line between two points in a plane is always a straight line, and that light in a homogeneous medium always takes the shortest (or at least locally shortest) path.

On a curved surface, however, there are in general no straight lines. Even for simple surfaces such as the sphere, cylinder, and cone, it is not immediately obvious what the shortest paths are, and for more complicated surfaces it is much more difficult to obtain an answer.

We shall first consider the problem of shortest lines on three surfaces S of rotation; the cylinder, the cone, and the sphere.

The cylinder surface contains straight lines, its meridians (the lines which generate it as a surface of revolution), and they certainly are lines of shortest connection.

What is the shortest connection of two points on these surfaces?

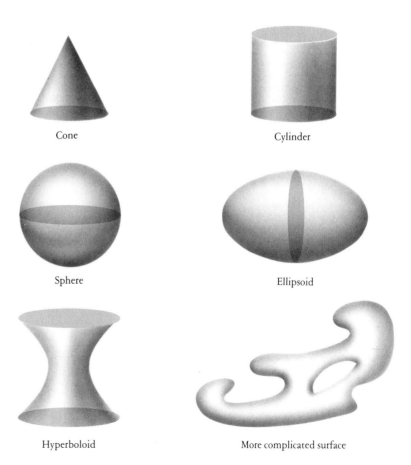

Cone

Cylinder

Sphere

Ellipsoid

Hyperboloid

More complicated surface

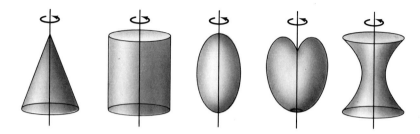

Various surfaces of revolution.

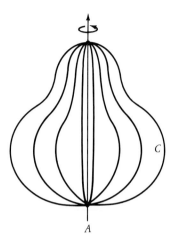

A meridian generating a surface of revolution.

Let us explain the important notion of a *meridian*. Imagine that a plane curve *C*, situated on one side of an axis *A*, is rotated about *A*, thereby generating a surface of revolution, as shown at the left. The various positions of *C* during this process are called the "meridians" of the surface of revolution. They are the generating curves of this surface. For instance, in this way a semicircle generates a sphere, a straight line parallel to the axis of rotation generates a cylinder, and half an ellipse produces an ellipsoid. Other possibilities are depicted above.

For a cylinder, any pair of points on a meridian has a straight line as shortest path of connection on the cylinder surface *S*. What are we going to do if two points *P* and *Q* do *not* lie on the same meridian? In fact, this is no real problem. We just remember that we may unroll each cylinder into a plane; this is what every house painter does when he uses his roller. For our purpose, it is somewhat simpler if we imagine *S* as the skin of a sausage that we cut above *P* and below *Q* (see the illustration below) by two planes that meet the cylinder axis perpendicularly. The piece *S′* that we are left with will be sliced along a suitable meridian *M*. Now we may spread the sliced skin into a plane,

The shortest connection between two points on a cylinder.

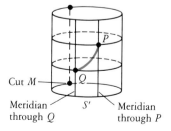

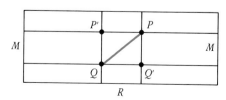

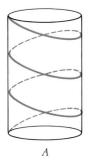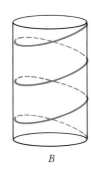

Helices: (A) left-handed; (B) right-handed.

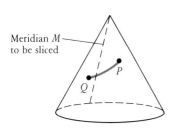

Meridian *M* to be sliced

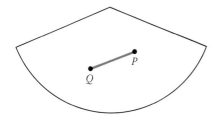

Shortest line on a cone.

where it takes the shape of a rectangle, *R*. Thus every line on *S'* is carried over into some line on *R*, and vice versa. Because we did not distort the skin *S'* in spreading it into the plane, we have not changed the length of any curve; hence this mapping of *S'* onto *R* is called an *isometric mapping*. For this reason, a shortest path on *S'* corresponds to a shortest path on *R*. Yet all shortest paths on *R* are known to us: they are straight lines. Now if we reverse our operation and roll *R*, like a peel, back over the sausage, the straight lines are transformed into helices or into circles (which are crushed helices) or into straight lines. Thus the shortest connection of *P* and *Q* on *S* is part of a helix—that is, of the line of a screw, as shown at the left. This is a curve that occurs quite often in nature.

We find a very similar situation if we study the shortest lines on a cone. Notice that each cone can be unrolled onto a planar domain; in fact, by cutting it along a meridian, we can spread it without distortion onto a portion of a plane. Again we employ the fact that the shortest lines in a plane are straight lines. This will immediately tell us what the shortest lines on *S* are. We need only to roll the planar image of *S* back onto the cone.

We may proceed similarly if we want to find the shortest lines on a polyhedron. By slicing it at some of its edges, we can again spread it out onto a plane without distortion.

However, the situation is quite different for most surfaces, including the sphere. Just try to spread any part of a sphere—say, the rubber hull of a ball—onto a planar domain. You will realize that you cannot do so without stretching the rubber.

There is a mathematical proof that no part of the sphere can be mapped without distortion onto a plane. This proof is based on a concept of curvature of a surface introduced by Carl Friedrich Gauss, now called the *Gaussian curvature*. This curvature measures precisely how curved a surface is at each of its points. (A definition of this notion will be given in Chapter 5.) Gauss's celebrated theorem then states that we can compute this curvature if we know the length of each curve on the surface. A somewhat more precise statement of Gauss's result is that the metric (that is, the measurement of length) determines the Gaussian curvature of the surface.

To see that a sphere cannot be mapped onto a planar domain without distortion, we compute the Gaussian curvature of a sphere of radius *R* to be of the same value, namely, $1/R^2$, at each of its points, whereas that of a planar domain is zero. If there were such a length-preserving map, it would follow that $1/R^2 = 0$, which is, of course, absurd.

Carl Friedrich Gauss (1777–1855).

This important result of Gauss he called *theorema egregium* (that is, remarkable theorem). It is the central result of his *Disquisitiones circa superficies curvas*, published in 1827, and it is valued as one of the most important discoveries in mathematics. It explained why we cannot make perfect charts of the surface of our planet: the search for charts on which lengths are uniformly proportional to the lengths on the globe is futile. Each type of projection used for chart making must have some disadvantages. We can choose only between various kinds of errors that the chart will have. Yet there is one property that maps can have. Map makers can find representations of the globe in which angles between lines (if not their lengths) are preserved. The Mercator projection provides just such a *conformal map*.

Even though unrolling will not work for the sphere, we can nevertheless find all its shortest lines. They must be portions of great circles on the sphere, because the sphere is symmetric in every direction, and because each meridian of a surface of revolution furnishes a shortest connection between any two of its points.

The first paper on the shortest line between two points *on a general surface* was published by Euler. This paper appeared under the title *De linea brevissima in superficie quacunque duo quaelibet puncta jungente* ("On the shortest line on an arbitrary surface connecting any two points whatsoever") in the *Commentarii of the Imperial Academy of St. Petersburg*, in the issue of 1728, which, however, was not publicly distributed until 1732.* Euler stated that we can easily solve the problem of shortest connection between two points on a convex surface by a simple mechanical artifice: we fix a string at one of the points and pull it taut in the direction of the other (see the left-hand drawing in the upper illustration on the next page). The string then yields the shortest connection between the two points.

Obviously this method does not work for a concave surface (see the right-hand figure); so Euler developed a new technique for finding the shortest line. He reduced the problem to the solution of a differential equation. This equation is equivalent to a geometric theorem derived (but not published) by Johann Bernoulli in 1698, in which he stated that *at each point P of a shortest line C, the corresponding osculating plane of C intersects the tangent plane to the surface at P in a right angle* (see the middle illustration).

---

*For some time, historians believed that this paper was incorrectly dated, and that Euler could not have submitted it for publication before 1729. Recent investigations seem, however, to indicate that the paper may have been written by the end of the year 1728.

A tight string between two points on a convex and a concave surface.

A. The tangent plane at *P.*
B. The osculating plane at *P* for geodesic curve *C.*

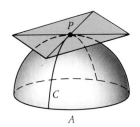

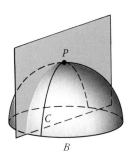

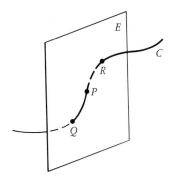

Three points *P, Q, R* on a curve determine a plane *E* that approximates the osculating plane.

What is this *osculating plane* that appears in Bernoulli's theorem? Take any two other points, *Q* and *R*, on *C* close to *P*. In general, the three points *P, Q,* and *R* will determine a plane. Of course, this plane will depend on *Q* and *R;* but if these points both move on *C* toward *P*, the plane will approach a limiting position, and this is called the *osculating plane to C at point P*.

Later on, the name *geodesic line*—or, briefly, *geodesic*—was given to all curves *C* on a surface *S* for which at each of their points *P*, the osculating plane to *C* and the tangent plane to *S* are perpendicular to each other. Then Bernoulli's theorem states that *curves of shortest length must be portions of geodesic lines.*

It turns out that "sufficiently small" portions of a geodesic always yield a shortest connection of their end points; but in general "large parts" will not have this minimizing property. For instance, on a sphere, all the geodesics are parts of great circles. Then, for any pair of points *P* and *Q* that are not at opposite ends of a diameter of the sphere (like the North and South Poles on the Earth), there is exactly one great circle passing through *P* and *Q*. The two points therefore decompose the circle into two arcs, of which the shorter one is the shortest line between *P* and *Q* and the other is geodesic but not a

Two points on a surface can sometimes be connected by more than one geodesic.

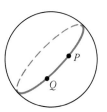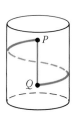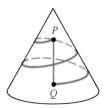

shortest connection (see above). The same figure also shows points P and Q on a cylinder and on a cone; both pairs are connected by a shortest line, as well as by a geodesic that is not minimal in length.

Complete surfaces, such as the sphere, the ellipsoid, and the cylinder, are defined as surfaces on which you can move with constant speed forever on every geodesic without ever leaving the geodesic. You might return to your point of departure, as on a sphere, or you might never return, as when you move along a helix on a cylinder. We have to emphasize the fact that Euler did not prove the existence of a shortest connection between two points on a complete surface. He only gave conditions that must be satisfied by such a line. The existence of a shortest connection was not proved until 1900 by David Hilbert.

The study of geodesics had a turbulent beginning. Johann Bernoulli, in August 1697, publicly posed the problem of finding the shortest line between two given points on a convex surface. This was meant as a challenge to his brother Jakob, with whom he was publicly feuding. The unfortunate rivalry of the two brothers eventually became so intense, and their polemics so ugly, that the scientific journals of the time declined to publish them. Let us look at the background of this feud, one of many scientific rivalries.

Between 1666 and 1680, Newton and Leibniz had discovered the infinitesimal calculus. It seems to be proved that both found this powerful mathematical technique independently. However, Newton's method was not published until 1711, whereas Leibniz had his basic ideas printed in the *Acta Eruditorum* of Leipzig, the first paper appearing in 1684. The publications of Leibniz were rather short and cryptic, and the first to understand them was Jakob Bernoulli, who in 1687 had become professor of mathematics at Basel. Jakob taught his younger brother, Johann, some of the secrets of the infinitesimal calculus, which he had rediscovered without any help from Leibniz. Thus, by 1690, Newton, Leibniz, and the two Bernoulli brothers were the only people who could handle the differential and integral calculus. Apparently at this time, the competition between the two brothers began.

David Hilbert (1862–1943) was a leading mathematician of his time.

Johann's challenge to find the shortest line between two points on a surface was met by Jakob, who in 1698 solved the problem for all surfaces of revolution. The restriction to these surfaces had originally been proposed by Johann himself at the time he stated the problem. Johann approved of the results of his brother, but criticized them as too special because Jakob had treated only the surfaces of revolution. In his paper Johann announced that he had found the solution of the shortest connection problem for an arbitrary surface. Was Johann's claim really justified? A letter of Johann to Leibniz, written in August 1698, seems to confirm his assertion. In this letter, he stated the "law of the osculating plane." Leibniz quickly replied, praising Johann's solution. About thirty years later, in December 1727, Johann again posed the problem of shortest connection, this time to his student Euler, and this is what led to Euler's 1728 paper. The appearance of Euler's paper did not keep Johann from attempting to reassert his priority over the solution to the shortest connection problem. In 1742 he claimed to have communicated the solution by letter to his colleague Klingenstierna in 1728.

Johann's claim, which nowadays is accepted, was long doubted, and you may wonder why. His boasting nature and underdeveloped sense of generosity certainly played a role. The affair connected with the publication of l'Hospital's calculus book also shed doubts on Johann's veracity. This is what happened. In 1691-92, on the occasion of a tour abroad, Johann met the Marquis de l'Hospital, the best French mathematician of the time. In exchange for a considerable financial pension, Johann pledged to communicate all his newest discoveries in the infinitesimal calculus to the Marquis and to remain silent about their deal during l'Hospital's lifetime. The Marquis transformed Johann's communications into the first textbook on the differential calculus, which appeared in 1696. Johann was not pleased, but, because of their prior agreement, said nothing. Only after the death of the Marquis and without mentioning his deal with l'Hospital did he claim priority over a part* of this book. People then became suspicious, and the reputation of this great but money-loving mathematician certainly suffered. In 1921, Johann's manuscript on the differential calculus was discovered. Together with the correspondence of l'Hospital and Bernoulli, it proved that the Swiss mathematician was the true author of l'Hospital's calculus book.

---

*The celebrated l'Hospital's rule for finding the value of expressions of the form 0/0.

Even more important than the shortest-connection problem was another question raised by Johann in June 1696. It was to become known as "the problem of quickest descent" or "the brachystochrone problem":

> For two given points A and B in a vertical plane, find a line connecting them on which a movable point M descends from A to B under the influence of gravitation in the quickest possible way.

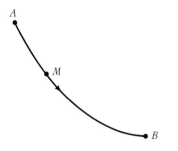

The problem of quickest descent.

You may think of a small, heavy ball that slides without friction in the shortest possible time on some track from A to B. What is the shape of this track? It certainly is not the straight line joining A and B. In 1638 Galileo had incorrectly claimed that the solution was a circular arc. What was the correct solution?

It turned out to be a well-known and, by this time, well-studied curve, not a circular arc but a line closely related to the circle: the *cycloid*—that is, the rolling curve of a circle—which we first met in Chapter 2.

The famous French mathematician Blaise Pascal studied the cycloid in 1649, when he was suffering from a painful toothache. To get some distraction, he began to investigate the rolling curve. When the pain disappeared, he took it as a sign that God was not displeased with his thoughts. Pascal's results stimulated other mathematicians to look at this curve, and subsequently numerous remarkable properties were found. The most interesting one was discovered by the Dutchman Christian Huygens.

Christian Huygens (1629–1695).

Huygens was probably most famous for his invention of the pendulum clock. In 1657 he obtained for this clock a patent from the Dutch states; yet Huygens was not content with his invention, because he realized that the time a pendulum would need to swing a full period was dependent on its amplitude. In other words, the circular pendulum was not isochronal; it did not always swing to and fro in the same amount of time, and this unfortunately led to irregularities in the

A cycloid.

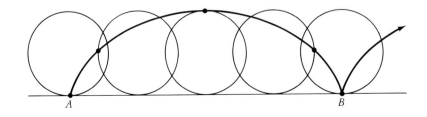

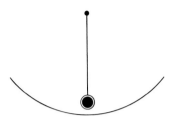

A circular pendulum.

The orbit of the tip of a pendulum.

The pendulum clock of Huygens. The pendulum swings between two cycloidal cheeks that are shown at the right.

clocks. So, Huygens asked, is there a *perfect pendulum?* If so, it should be constructed in such a way that the tip of the pendulum would swing on an *isochrone* (or *tautochrone*). This is a curve on which a frictionless point-mass would always move from any initial point A to the lowest point L of the curve in the same amount of time, regardless of what the height of A above L might be.

Huygens found that the isochronal curve was nothing but a cycloid. Thus the greatest clockmaker of all times, as he has been called, devised in his 1673 treatise *Horologium Oscillatorium* a pendulum clock the pendulum of which would swing on a cycloid. The apparatus is shown below.

The technical artifice was to use a flexible pendulum that swung between two cycloidal cheeks. This artifice was based on Huygens's beautiful mathematical insight that the *involute* of a cycloid is again a cycloid. This means the following. Imagine a flexible but unstretchable thread laid along an arc E of a cycloid that extends from A to B (see the drawing on the next page). Unwind the thread from E by pulling it tight, so that its loose end always extends tangentially away from curve

Fig. 2.

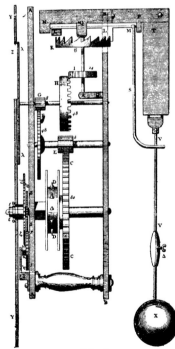

Fig. 1.

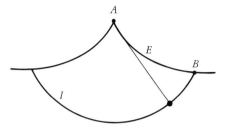

The perfect pendulum: the evolute of a cycloid is a cycloid.

Pierre de Fermat (1601–1665).

E. The end point *B* will describe a curve *I* that is called the *involute*, whereas *E* is called the *evolute* (from the Latin word *evolvere*, to unwind). Both the involute and the evolute of cycloids, then, are cycloids!

Thus we see that by 1697 the cycloid had been well studied, and so we can imagine how surprised mathematicians were to find that it was the very *brachystochrone* that Johann Bernoulli had challenged his brother Jakob to find.

In December 1696, Johann repeated his challenge in the *Acta Eruditorum*, asking for a solution by Easter 1697, and reported that Leibniz had already found one. In time, five mathematicians solved the problem; Johann and Jakob Bernoulli, Newton, Leibniz, and l'Hospital. Let us see how the problem of quickest descent was solved by Johann.

The main idea of his proof consisted in transforming the mechanical problem of quickest descent of a heavy point-mass into a problem of optics. Namely, Johann noticed that Galileo's law of a body falling along a certain curve meant that this body would move in the same way as a particle of light would in an atmosphere with a certain density that depended on height above the ground. Johann then used a result of the French mathematician Pierre de Fermat, a judge at the city of Toulouse and one of the greatest mathematicians of history. Fermat had found that the *law of refraction of light* follows from the assumption that *light always propagates in the quickest way from one point to another.* (This assumption is now called *Fermat's principle.*[*]) The law of refraction (in Fermat's time attributed to René Descartes, but now known to have been discovered by the Dutchman Willebrord Snell (1591–1626), says that the sines of the angles of refraction at a surface separating two homogeneous optical media are inversely proportional to the ratio of their densities, or

$$\frac{\sin \alpha_1}{\sin \alpha_2} = \frac{n_2}{n_1}.$$

The velocity of a particle of light in a medium is inversely proportional to the optical density of this medium.

Johann decomposed the atmosphere into very thin layers of constant density, applied the law of refraction, and then performed a limit procedure by letting the widths of the layers shrink to zero. This led to

---

[*]Heron's proof of the law of reflection is another application of Fermat's principle.

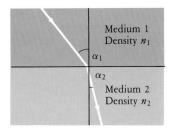

The law of refraction.

a differential equation for the curve of quickest descent, and Johann recognized that its solutions were cycloids.

It is remarkable that Johann Bernoulli had successfully connected the fields of optics and mechanics more than 100 years before the great Irish mathematician William R. Hamilton (1805–1865) was to develop his variational principles. These ideas eventually led to the unification of geometry and physics in present-day science.

DE
BEGHINSELEN
DER WEEGHCONST
BESCHREVEN DVER
SIMON STEVIN
van Brugghe.

WONDER EN IS GHEEN WONDER

TOT LEYDEN,
Inde Druckerye van Christoffel Plantijn,
By Françoys van Raphelinghen.
cIↃ. IↃ. LXXXVI.

4

A Miracle and Not a Miracle

Namely, because the shape of the whole universe is most perfect and, in fact, designed by the wisest creator, nothing in all of the world will occur in which no maximum or minimum rule is somehow shining forth.

Leonhard Euler

Notice the inscription *WONDER EN IS GHEEN WONDER*, which means "a miracle and not a miracle," in the emblem on the facing page. This emblem appeared on the title page of a work by the Dutch engineer Simon Stevin (1548–1620) and refers to his celebrated solution of an old mechanical problem.

Stevin wanted to know how much pull is needed to keep a weight that lies on an inclined plane in equilibrium (see the illustration at the top of the next page). Clearly no force is needed if the plane is horizontal, because it then carries the load, and the greatest pull is required when the plane is vertical. Thus these two cases are the extremes, and the general case is somewhere in between: the force necessary to balance the load will depend on the angle of inclination.

What is the precise rule? Stevin found the answer by looking at a slightly more general problem. He considered a prism of height h the base of which lies on the ground and is supposed to be perfectly horizontal. Assume that the prism has a triangular cross section ABC (see

Load on a horizontal plane, on a wall, and on an inclined plane.

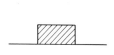 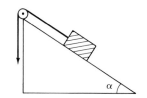

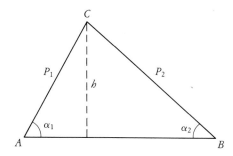

Cross section of a prism.

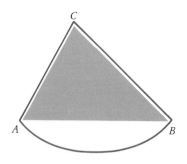

A prism with a chain around it.

the illustration at the left). The faces of the prism are formed by two planes, P_1 and P_2, which form angles α_1 and α_2, respectively, with the horizontal ground. Then two loads of weights m_1 and m_2 on P_1 and P_2, respectively, balance each other if and only if

$$\frac{m_1}{m_2} = \frac{\sin \alpha_2}{\sin \alpha_1}.$$

This is the law of the inclined plane, the proof of which appears on Stevin's emblem.

Here is Stevin's reasoning. Consider a closed chain of uniform thickness and density that surrounds the prism. Then, Stevin argues, either the chain is in equilibrium or it is moving. If it is moving, then the chain must be in permanent movement, because nothing else happens. This, however, Stevin thought to be impossible. Hence the chain is in equilibrium. The part of the chain below side AB will also be in equilibrium, because it hangs freely without support. Therefore the upper parts AC and BC of the chain balance each other. Their weights m_1 and m_2 are proportional to the distances $\overline{AC}$ and $\overline{BC}$; therefore

$$\frac{m_1}{m_2} = \frac{\overline{AC}}{\overline{BC}}.$$

On the other hand, we can find from the upper figure in the margin that

$$h = \overline{AC} \cdot \sin \alpha_1 \qquad \text{and} \qquad h = \overline{BC} \cdot \sin \alpha_2.$$

Therefore,

$$m_1 : m_2 = \sin \alpha_2 : \sin \alpha_1.$$

If we now replace the parts AC and BC of the chain by weights m_1 and m_2, they will balance each other as well.

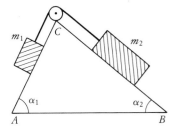

A prism supporting two loads.

Pulley from the Manesse manuscript (about 1330, University of Heidelberg).

This reasoning by Stevin is truly remarkable, since it reduces a difficult problem to a nearly obvious statement. The line of thought is quite in the tradition of Archimedes. Stevin was indeed one of the first since antiquity who had read and understood Archimedes' work on statics and hydraulics, and his main work was a modernization of the Archimedean ideas.

Only two of Archimedes' contributions to mechanics were handed down to us. They were called *On Floating Bodies* and *On the Equilibrium of Planes or Centers of Gravity of Plane Figures.* Both of them were published for the first time in 1543 by Nicolo Tartaglia (1506–1557), an Italian mathematician, just in time for Stevin. In his *Equilibrium*, Archimedes left the realm of pure mathematics for that of applied science. He derived a theory of equilibrium for mechanical configurations, based on seven axioms that he placed at the very beginning, thus doing the same for mechanics as Euclid had done for geometry. In this way he was the first to establish a mathematical theory for a part of physics, an accomplishment that was to become of great importance for the further development of science.

In the *Equilibrium*, Archimedes dealt with the lever, which, together with the wedge, inclined plane; roller, and pulley, belonged to the simple machines used in antiquity. (These machines enabled the classical cultures to erect such astounding constructions as the pyramids in Egypt, the Greek temples, and the Roman aqueducts.) He freely used the concept of the barycenter, or center of gravity, but never gave an explicit definition of this notion.[*] Pappus of Alexandria in about A.D. 340 gave the following explanation (which certainly is correct for convex bodies, though unsatisfactory in general):

We say that the center of gravity of any body is a point within that body such that, if the body were suspended from the point, the weight carried thereby remains at rest and preserves its original position.

With this idea, scientists like Stevin and Galileo started anew, about 1,800 years after Archimedes' death, to build a theory of *statics,*

---

[*]There have been various speculations why Archimedes never defined what he meant by "center of gravity." Some scholars assume that the concept had already been defined, either by earlier scientists or by Archimedes himself in a work now lost. The matter is not decided, but we have to assume that the reader was supposed to know what the term "center of gravity" meant.

that is, of the equilibrium of complicated mechanical systems. Yet we should not assume that during the intervening centuries mechanical knowledge did not exist. On the contrary, Roman architects developed new concepts, like the arch and vault, that obviously needed a profound understanding of the principles of statics. Although arch and vault had been used by other cultures before, it was the Romans who perfected them.

One of the admirable buildings of ancient Rome is the Pantheon, built about 1,900 years ago. Originally dedicated as a temple to the seven planetary deities, it later became the Christian church of Santa Maria Rotonda. The main hall of the Pantheon consists of a circular cylinder, covered by a self-supporting cupola of about 140 feet in diameter, consisting of some kind of concrete. The diameter of this cupola was unsurpassed until the year 1890, and even the diameter of the dome of St. Peter's in Rome is about four feet smaller.

The Roman arches can best be admired in the aqueducts found in most countries that were under Roman rule. The purpose of these structures was, and still is, to carry water from the mountains to the cities. The Romans loved water and used it lavishly in fountains, public baths, and private households. Even today, the city of Rome has the greatest abundance of water of all urban settlements in the world, and her wonderful fountains are unique in their exuberance and beauty. It

The Pantheon in Rome.

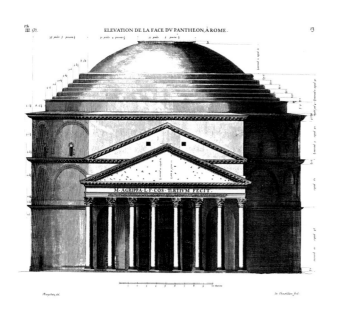

is astounding to think that 14 aqueducts led to the ancient city, some of them a hundred kilometers long; the few that still function suffice to provide the present city with all the water she needs.

The buildings erected in medieval Europe are possibly even more impressive and astounding than the Roman edifices. With the invention of the pointed arch, based on the ellipse, a new principle of construction was introduced. It permitted construction of the spectacular gothic cathedrals, much admired for their elegance and beauty.

When the ideas of Archimedes became widely known in Italy during the time of the Renaissance, Galileo and, in particular, Evangelista Torricelli (1608–1647) took up the Archimedean concept of the barycenter of a mechanical system. They stated the principle that such a system will be in (stable) equilibrium if its barycenter is as low as possible within the given limitations.

Johann and Jakob Bernoulli, who were to make the city of Basel a world center of mathematics, pondered what might be the equilibrium position of a heavy chain fixed at its end points. They decided that a chain is nothing but a mechanical system consisting of very many small, rigid parts, its links. Hence the equilibrium state should be characterized by the lowest position of its center of gravity. Once the chain has reached a configuration in which it cannot lower any link without in turn raising another, it will be in equilibrium. After

Equilibrium of a rectangular block: (A) stable position; (B) relatively stable position (that is, stable as long as dislocations are sufficiently small); (C) unstable, with no equilibrium; (D) unstable equilibrium; (E) another stable equilibrium.

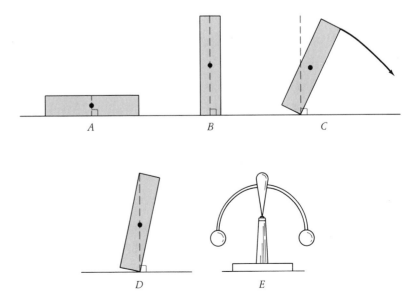

A ball on a hilly landscape.

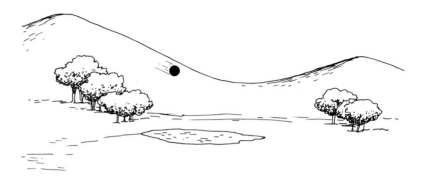

The catenary: the equilibrium position of a chain.

having formulated this principle, Johann Bernoulli in 1690 found the exact mathematical shape of the freely hanging chain, and so did Huygens and Leibniz. This shape is described by a curve that is nowadays called the *catenary* (mathematically, it is a *hyperbolic cosine*). We shall meet the catenary again later, in the chapter on minimal surfaces.

Great progress in the theory of equilibria of mechanical systems was made in 1717 by Johann Bernoulli, who proposed *the principle of virtual work** (which had already appeared in various contexts) as the fundamental law of statics. It states that

> in equilibrium, no work is needed to achieve an infinitesimal displacement of a given mechanical system.

This rule captures not only stable configurations, but also unstable ones. To see what this means, imagine a ball of steel that can roll on a landscape with depressions and elevations, as shown above. If the ball is on top of a hill, it lies in an unstable equilibrium; in the center of a pit, it is in a stable position. On the hill, any small kick will move the ball far away from its equilibrium position; in the pit, the ball tries to return to its site of rest, whatever the kicking direction may have been. If, however, the ball lies on a saddle, it is in an unstable equilibrium position. There are directions of no return, yet there are also directions in which the ball may undergo an oscillatory motion after receiving a

---

*This principle was stated in a letter by Johann Bernoulli to the French physicist Pierre Varignon (1654–1722), written January 26, 1717. It was first published in Varignon's *Nouvelle Mécanique*, vol. 2, p. 174, in 1725.

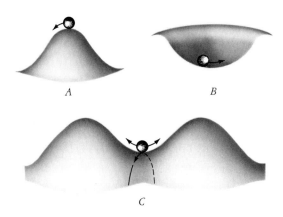

Various equilibrium positions of a ball:
(*A*) unstable; (*B*) stable; and (*C*) unstable.

slight kick. No work is needed (at least in first approximation) to move the ball slightly from any of the three equilibrium positions, because at these points gravity acts perpendicularly to the tangent planes to the surface and is therefore completely balanced by the reacting force of the ground.

It is not easy to formulate the principle of virtual work in general without employing some mathematics; yet we can recast the principle in such a way that its basic idea can be explained without too many mathematical technicalities. Let us suppose that a number is attached to each state of a physical system; this number is its *potential energy.* We can therefore consider the potential energy to be a function of the various states of the system. Then the principle of virtual work can be expressed by the following two rules, which mathematicians often call *Dirichlet's principle.*

> RULE 1. The stable equilibrium states (that is, states of rest) of a physical system are characterized by the condition that, in such a state, the potential energy of the system is less than it would be for any possible (or virtual) close-by state of the system.

To get a rough geometric picture of what this means, let us imagine the set of all possible states of a physical system to be a plane, each *point in the plane* representing a possible *state.* If we think of potential energy as the *height* of a mountain range over the plane, then the minima of the range (the pits) correspond to stable equilibria. At these points the tangent plane of the mountain range is horizontal.

As we already know, there are other points that have horizontal tangent planes; these are the maxima (peaks) and the saddle points (passes) of the range. They are supposed to correspond to the *unstable* states of rest. Generally we call the states that correspond to the points of the mountain range with a horizontal tangent plane the *stationary states* of the potential energy. Then we can state the second rule as follows.

> RULE 2. The equilibrium states of a physical system are the stationary states of its potential energy.

This geometric picture yields a simple mathematical framework in which to study equilibria of a physical system. The infinitesimal calculus allows us to precisely define the horizontal tangent planes of the multidimensional mountain ranges that we encounter in physics. Then we can use the methods of the calculus of variations to locate and characterize the equilibrium states. The unstable equilibria are as important as the stable ones. However, in most physical theories the basic equations characterize the equilibrium states only in general, whereas considerations of stability usually are a difficult matter.

There is, of course, another crucial question: *What potential energy should be assigned to each state of a physical model?* It is here that physical and experimental evidence enter. In order to obtain some feel for the concept of potential energy, let us consider some simple models, but in these models we will not be specific about what the exact potential energy is.

If you are a skier and you gain some height in the mountains, either by taking a lift or by walking upward, you also gain potential energy. On top of the mountain you will be in unstable equilibrium. A slight movement starts your race downward. During this race your potential energy is transformed first into kinetic energy and then, by friction, into heat energy. Once you have reached the valley, you will be in a stable position of minimal potential energy. However, if you climb a mountain pass with your skis, you will be at an intermediate unstable equilibrium position, at neither a maximum nor a minimum of the potential energy.

Another example is provided by an elastic medium, say, by the spring of a clock. Such a spring can store a certain amount of energy. As you wind the clock, kinetic energy is transformed into potential energy, which is stored by the spring and slowly released as the clock ticks. When the spring has lost its tension, it will be in stable equilibrium, and the clock will be at rest.

Similarly, if you squeeze an elastic object like a rubber ball or a rubber ring, you load it with potential energy, which the body would release if it were not for the counterforce exerted by your hands. Once you leave the rubber alone, it will try to lose as much of its potential energy as possible, by reshaping to its original position of least potential energy.

If you cut a rubber ring, twist one end, and glue the ends back together, the ring will now contain interior tensions, which it tries to release when it is left free. As a result you will get an equilibrium position that is rather different from the original one.

Still other models can be obtained by loading a system of springs with a heavy weight. The elastic forces of the springs will counteract the weight force exerted by gravity. Once more, equilibrium is achieved if the potential energy of the system is as small as possible.

You might replace the springs by a rubber cloth that spans a frame, and place on it some heavy substance, such as a stone or, even

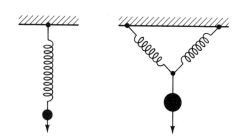

Springs balancing weights.

Rubber cloth carrying a stone or water.

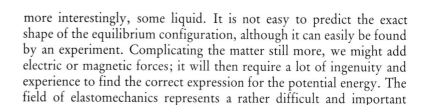

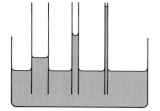

Capillary tubes of varying sizes.

Sessile and pendant drops.

more interestingly, some liquid. It is not easy to predict the exact shape of the equilibrium configuration, although it can easily be found by an experiment. Complicating the matter still more, we might add electric or magnetic forces; it will then require a lot of ingenuity and experience to find the correct expression for the potential energy. The field of elastomechanics represents a rather difficult and important topic in applied mathematics, one that is by no means complete despite the important achievements of many great mathematicians and physicists of the eighteenth and nineteenth centuries.

The rubber with the liquid on top is related to a phenomenon we encounter every day: the phenomenon of capillarity. Leonardo da Vinci observed in 1490 the rising and falling of liquids in small tubes, the capillary tubes. This phenomenon lent its name to the theory of surface tension, which is commonly called *the theory of capillarity*. Why do drops of water hang from a surface, as long as they are not too large? In the common explanation of this phenomenon, we imagine that the surface of each liquid is covered by an elastic skin. This skin balances the weight of the water droplet by its elastic properties, as the

rubber sheet did with the liquid. This explanation is a good one, because it is conceptually very simple, and because it can be justified by many experiments. For example, you have probably seen the water beetle, which can run on top of the surface of a pool. It walks on the skin of the water.

The British writer Hilaire Belloc described the water beetle's particular talent as follows:

The WATER BEETLE here shall teach
A sermon far beyond your reach:
He flabbergasts the Human Race
By gliding on the water's face
With ease, celerity, and grace;
But if he ever stopped to think
Of how he did it, he would sink.

The surface tension of water depends very much on the kind and amount of minerals dissolved in it. In some parts of the world, the surface tension of the water is so strong that it can support a small coin. High surface tension makes it much more difficult to wash your hands or to clean your laundry. The basic purpose of detergents is to drastically reduce the surface tension of water used in washing machines.

However, it is the reduction of surface tension by soap or by other detergents that enables us to produce soap films, which can either be held by a framework consisting of wires, threads, and surfaces or exist without a boundary, in the form of a soap bubble. Without the soap to reduce the tension, a liquid film of water could not persist, but would immediately break.

A precise explanation of surface tension in terms of the action of molecular forces is not easy. Moreover, it must take other phenomena into account—for example, the vapor layer covering a liquid surface. Yet the beautiful and simple concept of characterizing stable equilibrium states as minima of potential energy will enable us to explain the behavior of soap films quite satisfactorily. Because a liquid skin behaves in many ways like an elastic rubber cloth, it should have higher potential energy the more it is stretched. That is, the stored energy of a liquid surface should be related in some way to its area; the simplest rule is for potential energy to be in direct proportion to area. Thus a

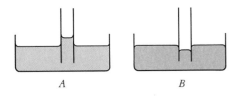

Capillary surfaces: (*A*) water; (*B*) mercury. These demonstrate the attracting and repelling forces exerted by the sides of a vessel upon a fluid.

soap film will be in stable equilibrium if its area is less than that of any other surface satisfying the same restrictions.

For a liquid drop, the potential energy is more complicated. It depends on the area of the free surface, the gravitational potential of the droplet, and the potential of the forces exerted by the boundary on the liquid. The boundary forces can be either pulling, as between glass and water, or repelling, as between glass and mercury. This approach, which is based on Johann Bernoulli's principle of virtual work, was used by Gauss in his paper *Principia generalia theoriae fluidorum in statu equilibrii* ("General principles of the theory of fluids in equilibrium"), which appeared in 1830. In this work Gauss put the theory of capillarity that had been proposed by P. S. Laplace in the tenth volume of his famous treatise *Mécanique céleste* (*Celestial Mechanics*, 1806) on a solid basis.

Gauss's work has important consequences. It allows us to describe the equilibrium positions of soap films as surfaces that, for given boundary configurations, assume a minimum area among all virtual (possible) positions or are at least stationary states of the area. Thus we have arrived at the theory of minimal surfaces; we shall exhibit some of its highlights in the next chapter.

5

Soap Films: The Amusement
of Children and Mathematicians

*The book of nature is written
in the characters of geometry.*

(Galileo Galilei)

Like the boy in the 1739 painting by
the French artist Chardin, most of us have at one time or another
blown soap bubbles. We prepared a soap solution, dipped a straw into
the liquid, withdrew it, and then blew some bubbles.

Bubble blowing is an old pastime. There is even an Etruscan vase
in the Louvre, on which children are portrayed blowing bubbles.
Nowadays special bubble solutions can be purchased; they come with
a simple wire frame and handle. When this frame is dipped into the
liquid and then withdrawn, a disclike soap film is formed. Blowing
into the frame creates a bubble.

If we replace the circular frame by one of a more complicated
geometric shape, made of thin flexible wire, very beautiful soap films
of a bizarre and interesting form will appear. Soon the films will show
iridescent colors produced by interference effects. After some time,
however, the film may get so thin that it actually becomes invisible.

A boy blowing a soap bubble (painting by
Chardin).

Soap Films and Minimal Surfaces: The Problem of Plateau

The fascinating laminae that appear in soap-film experiments are obviously in stable equilibrium; so they must be what are called *laminae of minimal potential energy* that span the wire frame, as follows from Johann Bernoulli's principle of virtual work that we discussed in the last chapter.

Consequently, since potential energy is proportional to area, the *mathematical surfaces* that model soap films are surfaces of least area or, as mathematicians say, minimal surfaces. A minimal surface has a smaller area than any *nearby surface* that spans the same frame. The marvellous shapes of soap films and of their mathematical models are visible and very striking examples of a minimum principle at work.

Mathematicians have long been attracted by minimal surfaces because of the interesting and challenging problems they pose. It was Lagrange, Euler's successor at the court of Frederic II, who in 1760 derived the celebrated *minimal surface equation* that we will state later on. The extensive experimental and theoretical work on the phenomenon of capillarity by the Belgian physicist J. A. P. Plateau included fascinating experiments on liquid films that stimulated the interest of mathematicians. In 1873 Plateau published a large part of his observations, measurements, and theoretical insights in the treatise *Statique expérimentale et théoretique des liquides soumis aux seules forces moléculaires* (Experimental and theoretical statics of liquids subjected solely to molecular forces), his major work.

Plateau did not see many of his experiments; he lost his sight in 1843, because, during an experiment in physiological optics, he had stared at the Sun for longer than 25 seconds without protecting his eyes. In later years he therefore had to rely on the help of his family and of assistants when he wanted to carry out his investigations.

One of Plateau's observations was particularly important for mathematics. By numerous experiments he realized that every contour consisting of a single closed wire, whatever its geometric form (provided it is not too large), bounds at least one soap film. Does the corresponding statement hold for the mathematical models of soap films, the minimal surfaces? In other words, is it true that every closed curve in space can be spanned by at least one minimal surface? This *mathematical question* became known as the *Plateau problem*. Many famous mathematicians of the nineteenth and twentieth centuries were intrigued by this problem, but its solution appeared to be very difficult.

Joseph Antoine Ferdinand Plateau (1801–1883).

Richard Courant (1888–1972) and his student
Charles De Prima.

Despite the difficulty of the mathematical problem, the soap film, as Plateau observed, is a solution to the corresponding physical problem. However, as Richard Courant, one of the principal researchers on minimal surfaces in this century, has remarked,

Empirical evidence can never establish mathematical existence—nor can the mathematician's demand for existence be dismissed by the physicist as useless rigor. Only a mathematical existence proof can ensure that the mathematical description of a physical phenomenon is meaningful.

Let us consider an example that illustrates his point. Christian Goldbach (1690–1764) had noticed that even numbers greater than 4 seem to be the sum of two odd prime numbers (it is a mathematical convention that 1 is not a prime number, and 2 is, of course, the only even prime number):

$6 = 3 + 3$;	$16 = 3 + 13$;	$26 = 13 + 13$;
$8 = 5 + 3$;	$18 = 7 + 11$;	$28 = 5 + 23$;
$10 = 5 + 5$;	$20 = 7 + 13$;	$30 = 7 + 23$;
$12 = 7 + 5$;	$22 = 11 + 11$;	$32 = 3 + 29$;
$14 = 7 + 7$;	$24 = 5 + 19$;	$34 = 17 + 17$.

In a letter to Euler in 1742, Goldbach asked whether he could prove that this sequence can be continued *ad infinitum*. Euler was never able to do so, nor has anyone else up to the present day. Today's fastest computer can check the validity of Goldbach's conjecture for an enormously large number of even integers, but obviously it cannot verify it for all even integers, since there are infinitely many. Thus any checking procedure would require an infinite amount of time if all even numbers were to be tested.

This consideration provides a good reason why physical experiments can never prove a mathematical statement. No matter how many experiments you may carry out to verify a claim, you can never exclude the possibility that another repetition of the experiment might yield a different result. Hence empirical evidence can never establish a mathematical fact. Even for the physicist it is important to obtain a rigorous mathematical existence proof, because only thus can he verify beyond any doubt that his mathematical model of a physical situation is at least in some respect correct. Passing to a mathematical model of soap films necessitates that we speak of a curve instead of a wire and a surface instead of a soap film. Curves and surfaces are idealizations like those created by the ancient Greeks.

The mathematical definitions of curves and surfaces were developed during the late seventeenth and early eighteenth centuries by the Bernoullis, Leibniz, and, in particular, Euler. Their advantage over the Greeks was that, during the seventeenth century, René Descartes had created a powerful mathematical tool, *analytic geometry*, which expresses geometry in terms of numbers and equations. A planar curve, for example, is described by a single equation relating the variables x and y, which are plotted against each other on the familiar square grid. For example, the formula $x^2 + y^2 = a^2$ describes a circle of radius a centered at the point $x = 0$, $y = 0$. Subsequently it was not a great

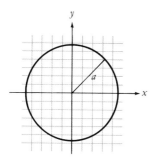

The equation $x^2 + y^2 = a^2$ describes a circle of radius a.

A   B   C

A closed curve that can be spanned by at least three different minimal surfaces

problem to define the concepts "length of a curve," "area of a surface," and "volume of a body" by means of the infinitesimal calculus, and to compute length, area, and volume of many interesting geometric objects. More or less the same definitions are still used and are studied every year by thousands of first-year university students.

The solutions of the Plateau problem can be of many different types. In order to get an idea of what may happen, let us consider a particular closed curve that can be spanned by at least three different minimal surfaces. In the figure at the left, the middle and right-hand surfaces are of the same type, but the left-hand one is of a different kind. Mathematicians say that the left-hand surface has *genus* 1, whereas the other two have *genus* 0. What does this mean?

To solve the Plateau problem, we need to know how complicated a surface spanning a contour can be. We thus need a way to classify the surfaces among which we might find a solution. A coarse but useful classification distinguishes between various *topological types*. Two surfaces are of the same topological type if you can deform one into the other by stretching as you would stretch an elastic membrane, allowing different parts of a surface to pass through one another (for example, see the illustration on page 161), but without any tearing, cutting, or gluing. Some surfaces of the same topological type as a sphere are shown below.

We may now cut out two discs from the sphere and attach a handle (see the upper figure on the next page). We can continue this process, attaching two, three, or more handles to the sphere. In this way we get a collection of finite surfaces without boundary, called *handle-body surfaces*, that are mutually distinct. If two such surfaces have a different number of attached handles, they are of different topological types (see the lower figure on the next page.)

Closed surfaces of the same topological type as the sphere.

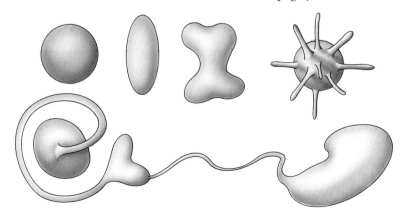

One handle being attached to a sphere.

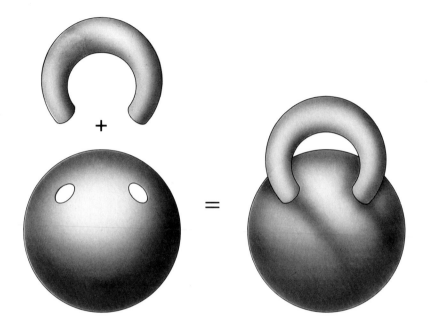

A sphere with 0,1,2,3 handles attached.

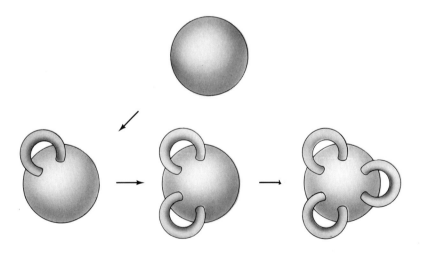

Surfaces of genus 1 (doughnut), genus 2 (pretzel), and the baker's pretzel.

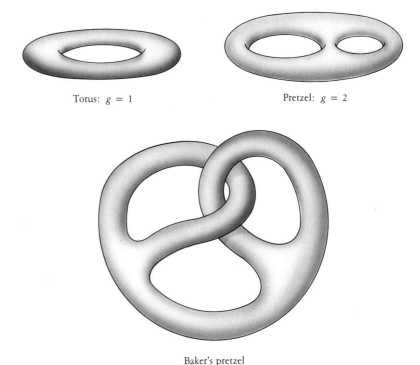

Torus: $g = 1$

Pretzel: $g = 2$

Baker's pretzel

Observe that stretching the sphere with one handle turns it into a torus, the surface of a doughnut; and the sphere with two handles is of the same type as the surface of a pretzel. Notice that the baker's pretzel above is of the same topological type as the sphere with two handles.

A surface is said to be of *genus g* if it is of the topological type of a sphere with g handles attached. Thus the torus has the genus 1, and 2 is the genus of the pretzel.

The surfaces that we have considered so far have not had any boundary. Now we may cut holes into them, say, m holes that are bounded by m curves $C_1, C_2, \ldots, C_m$. Two surfaces obtained in this way turn out to be of the same topological type if they have the same genus and the same number of holes. More specifically, we say that a surface with m holes in its skin has the genus g if, when we fill the holes with m disc-type surfaces, we create a surface without boundary and of the type of a sphere with g handles attached. We may call this object a handle-body surface of genus g with m holes.

Surfaces with (*A*) one hole but different
genus; (*B*) surface of genus 4 with 6 holes;
(*C*) sphere with two holes.

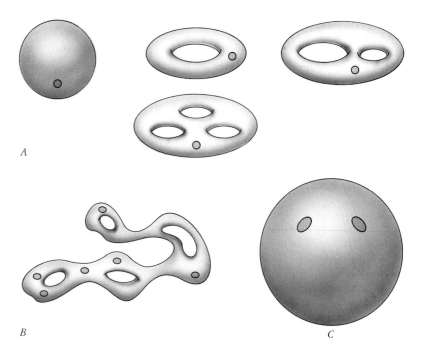

Let us now consider surfaces with exactly one hole. All of them
could, in principle, be of the same topological type as the solutions to
Plateau's problem. Indeed, it may very well happen that the same
curve may bound minimal surfaces of different topological types. For
example, surfaces *B* and *C* on page 95 have $g = 0$ and $m = 1$, whereas
surface *A* has $g = 1$ and $m = 1$.

We note that any surface of the type of a sphere with one hole
(that is, $g = 0$, $m = 1$) is of the same type as the disc (see the figure
below). The disc is the simplest possible surface whose boundary is formed

A sphere with one hole can be stretched into
a disc.

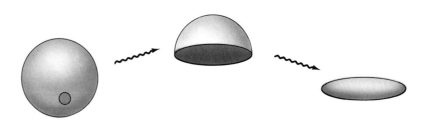

by a simple closed curve. Hence all the disc-type minimal surfaces within a given contour are in a way the simplest solutions to Plateau's problem.

A disc-type minimal surface may have an area smaller than that of any nearby surface or, in fact, any other disc surface; yet there may be a surface of higher genus with less area. In other words, a disc-type minimal surface may not be the surface of least area that spans a preassigned curve, but may furnish only a local minimum of area. An example of this phenomenon is displayed in the margin on page 95. (In order to make it very convincing, we should squeeze the two pairs of adjacent circlelike parts of the curve very close together.)

Thus for a given curve C it is not at all obvious which genus g will yield the surface of absolute minimum area spanning C. It is not even obvious if a minimum is achieved for any surface no matter what its genus is. For example, consider a pathological curve like the one in the upper illustration below. The absolute minimum of area is achieved by a surface that looks like the "Loch Ness monster," as depicted in the lower figure. This monster is not contained in our previous collection, because it is of the topological type of *a sphere with only one hole to which infinitely many handles are attached*. Therefore it is topologically nothing but a disc with infinitely many handles, as is shown in the top figure on the next page.

The boundary of the Loch Ness monster.

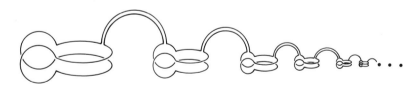

The Loch Ness monster.

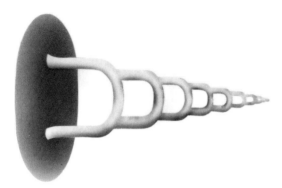

A disc with infinitely many handles.

This absurd example arises because we considered a contour that possesses a *singular point:* the very tip of the tail of the monster. Could it be that such unpleasant *surfaces of infinite genus cannot appear as solutions of the Plateau problem if we admit only "regular" smooth curves as possible contours?* This, in fact, has recently been proved.

Do minimal surfaces have other surprises waiting for us? Can we, for instance, expect to find all possible soap films that span a given contour in our collection of handle-body surfaces, or must we extend this list?

Let us consider the curve shown below. It is spanned by two surfaces *A* and *B* of different topological types; and, if the wire looks like that in the figure in the margin at the lower left, then a surface very similar to surface *A* will be the surface of least area that spans it. However, surface *A* is not contained in our collection of handle-body surfaces with *m* holes and with genus *g*, because all of these surfaces are two-sided, but *A* is one-sided. Two-sided means that the surface really has two sides, like surface *B*, so that a little animal walking on the surface can never move from one side to the other without crossing the boundary, but on a one-sided surface it can get everywhere without ever crossing the boundary.

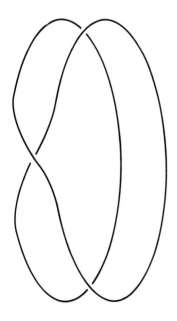

Two minimal surfaces spanning a closed curve.

The surface of least area spanning this curve is of the topological type of the Möbius strip.

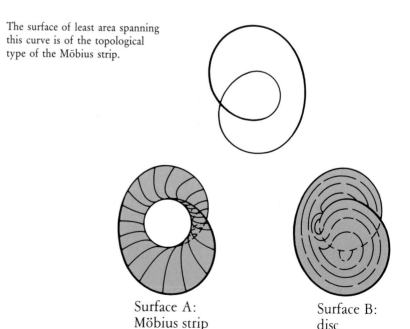

Surface A:
Möbius strip

Surface B:
disc

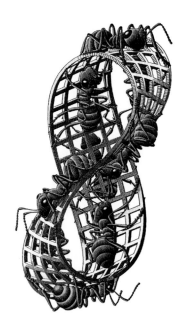

Möbius strip (by M.C. Escher).

August Ferdinand Möbius (1790–1868).

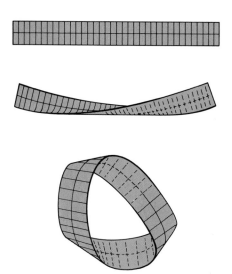

Generating a Möbius strip.

Surface *A* is of the same topological type as the celebrated *Möbius strip* discovered in 1858 by the German mathematician and astronomer A. F. Möbius, professor at Leipzig University. You can produce this strip by cutting a long strip of paper, twisting it once, and pasting its ends together. This surface indeed has only one side, as you can see either by producing it yourself or by studying the 1963 etching by the Dutch artist M. C. Escher, as shown at the left above.

Since the discovery of the Möbius strip, mathematicians have found a large set of different topological types of finite one-sided surfaces, with no hole, one hole, two holes, and so forth. However, many of them must have self-intersections, like the Klein bottle, named after the German mathematician Felix Klein (1849–1925). These surfaces are called *nonorientable*, because we cannot distinguish a clockwise from a counterclockwise rotation on such a surface (see the upper figures on the next page). Our collection of handle-body surfaces represents the set of orientable finite surfaces.

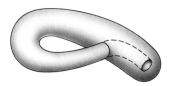

The Klein bottle has only one side: its inside is the same as its outside.

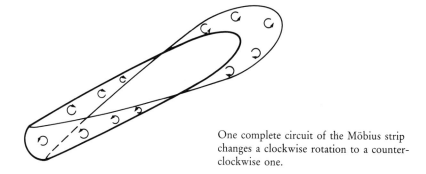

One complete circuit of the Möbius strip changes a clockwise rotation to a counter-clockwise one.

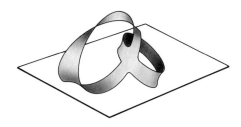

A nonorientable surface of genus 1 spanning a closed curve.

A nonorientable surface of genus 2 spanning a closed curve.

Finally, let us consider two one-sided minimal surfaces that are of more complicated topological types than the Möbius strip. The figures at the left show that it is far from obvious what the topological type of a potential solution to the Plateau problem should be. However, we have already seen that surfaces of the type of the disc are among the simplest surfaces that can span a closed curve. Thus we pose the following question:

> Can we prove that there exists at least one surface of the type of the disc having a minimum area within the class of all disc-type surfaces that span a given simple closed curve?

(A *simple* curve is one that does not intersect itself, like a circle and unlike a figure eight.)

During the nineteenth century, this disc version of the Plateau problem was solved for many special curves, mostly polygons, and many special minimal surfaces were discovered. The achievements of mathematicians like Riemann, Weierstrass, and Schwarz were of first rank; nevertheless, the tools available to them did not suffice to tackle the Plateau problem in general. In 1914, the French geometer Gaston Darboux (1842–1917) observed: *"Until now, mathematical analysis has not been able to invent any method that will permit us to begin with the investigation of this beautiful question."*

In 1928, a young American mathematician, Jesse Douglas, solved the disc version of the Plateau problem. In the same year, he lectured about his solution at the University of Göttingen in Germany, by that time one of the principal scientific and mathematical centers of the world. Apparently not all of Douglas's arguments were convinc-

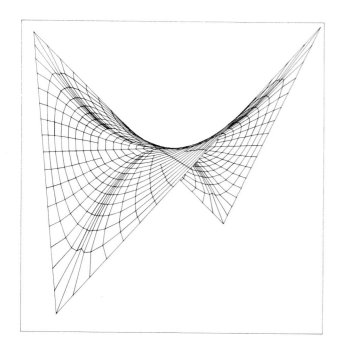 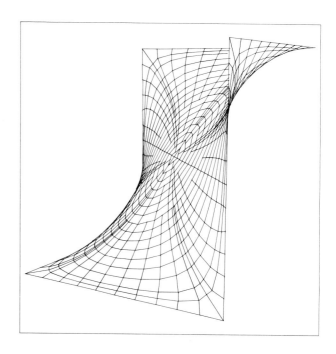

Computer-generated drawings of two of Schwarz's solutions to Plateau's problem for polygons.

ing, and the audience had doubts about the completeness of his proof. It took Douglas two more years to fill in the details, and his work did not appear until 1931. By that time a totally different proof devised by the Hungarian mathematician Tibor Radó had been published.

During the following decade, Jesse Douglas solved many other problems for minimal surfaces. His powerful methods permitted him to treat existence questions for minimal surfaces of higher genus spanning one or even finitely many closed curves. For his accomplishments, he was awarded in 1936 one of the first two Fields medals in mathematics. (Nobel prizes are not awarded in mathematics, and the Fields medal is the highest award offered by the International Congress of Mathematicians.)

The work of Douglas and Radó did not end the study of minimal surfaces. Many other beautiful results have been obtained since then, as we shall see. One of the most important achievements has been the solution of the general Plateau problem. It has now been proved that, *for each simple closed curve, there exists a surface of least area and of finite genus spanning this contour; furthermore, this least-area surface will not have self-intersections.* From this, we infer that for knotted curves the least-area surface cannot be a disc.

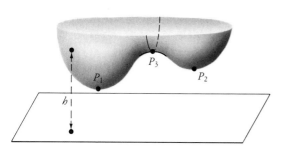

Deformed bowl.

Computer-generated drawings of (A and B) stable minimal surfaces; and (C) of "Enneper's surface," an unstable-equilibrium surface, which represents a phantom soap film.

A Geometric Description of Minimal Surfaces

In the preceding section, we used the term "minimal surfaces" for the minima of area—that is, for the mathematical models of stable soap films. In soap films, the potential energy of the "surface tension" is at a local minimum.

We have seen that a given closed curve may bound more than one "stable" minimal surface. It is then natural to ask if there exist surfaces spanning a given contour that correspond to *unstable equilibria of potential energy*.

Let us illustrate the situation by a mechanical analogue: a deformed steel bowl, as depicted at the left. Here we have two minimum points P_1 and P_2 for the height h above a fixed plane, and a point P_3 of unstable equilibrium.

Consider now a closed contour that can be spanned by two different disc surfaces that are relative minima of area. Then we can ask whether there is a third surface yielding an unstable equilibrium of area that would correspond to point P_3, the unstable equilibrium. If so, can we find a *geometric condition* that describes both stable and unstable equilibria of area? In both cases, the answer is "yes." The existence of two minima of area indeed require the existence of a disc surface that is an unstable equilibrium of area. You cannot see the corresponding soap film, because it is a fleeting ghost that may appear for only a fraction of a second when you flip one minimum into the other. A picture of such a phantom soap film is shown at the right below.

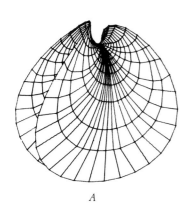

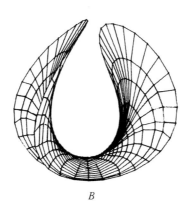

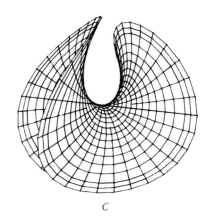

A   B   C

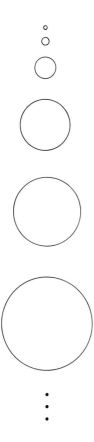

Circles of increasing radius.

How can we formulate a condition that will characterize all equilibrium surfaces, stable or unstable, in the same way? Everyone knows that a straight line does not curve; indeed, this is a tautology. If we were asked to assign a value to the amount of curviness of a straight line, the answer would, of course, be zero. But what about other curves; how curvy are they?

Let us begin to answer this question by first considering a circle of radius r. A circle curves the same amount at every point. If r is small, then the circle is very curvy. As the radius r increases, the circle becomes larger and larger, and it curves less and less. We would like a definition of curvature that reflects this simple observation. We therefore *define* the curvature κ (a Greek kappa) of a circle by the rule

$$\kappa = \frac{1}{r} \quad \text{or} \quad \text{curvature} = \frac{1}{\text{radius}}.$$

Thus as the radius r gets larger, the curvature κ gets smaller.

Then, what do we do with a more complicated plane curve, like the one below (part A)? It is obvious that this curve is at some places very curvy, and at others it doesn't curve at all. If a number can be assigned that measures curviness, this number will therefore change as we move from point to point on the curve. Let us take an arbitrary curve C, planar or not, and a point P on it (as shown in part B below).

If the curve is smooth, there will be tangent line T to the curve at point P. We can then show that there is a circle that passes through point P, that has the same tangent as that of curve C, and that "best fits" C at point P. The precise definition of this circle requires the infinitesimal calculus, but we can give a rough idea of it. Choose two points P_1 and P_2 close to P. Then the three points P_1, P_2, and P determine a circle. As P_1 and P_2 squeeze in toward P, this circle gets closer

A. A general curve.
B. Radius of curvature.

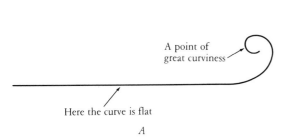

A point of
great curviness

Here the curve is flat

A

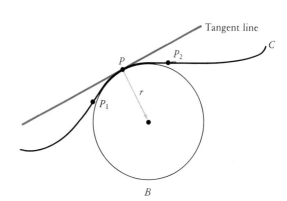

B

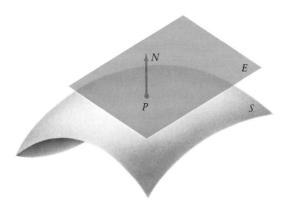

A surface S, a tangent plane E, a point P, and a normal direction N.

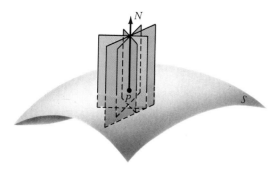

A bushel of normal planes at P determined by a normal direction N.

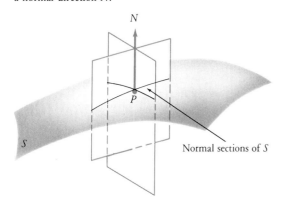

Two normal planes and their normal sections at P.

and closer to the best-fitting one. If r is the radius of this circle, then the curvature κ of C at P will be defined as $1/r$. For reasons that will soon become clear, we shall also give a sign to the curvature of certain curves that are called *normal sections of a surface*. That is, we shall define the curvature κ of a "normal section" as $1/r$ or as $-1/r$, according to a convention that we shall now describe.

First, what is a normal section? Let us consider an arbitrary surface S, as shown in the upper figure at the left. We fix a point P on this surface, and then we choose a direction N that is perpendicular to the tangent plane E that touches the surface S only at the point P. Such a perpendicular direction is called a *surface normal* of S at the point P. You may imagine such a normal N as an arrow that is fixed with its end at the point P (at each point of a regular surface there exist two normal arrows, pointing in opposite directions).

Finally, we consider a further plane, which passes through point P and contains the normal direction N, as shown in the middle figure at the left. We call it a *normal plane* to the surface at point P. Obviously, there can be infinitely many normal planes at P; you can find them all by revolving any such plane about the axis determined by the normal direction N.

Each normal plane at point P intersects the surface S in a plane curve that is called a *normal section of S*. Consider now a normal section C of the surface at point P, and let r be the radius of the best-fitting circle at P, as shown in the lower figure at the left. This circle lies in the same plane as the normal section C, and its center is situated on the straight line that contains the "normal arrow" N. Then either the arrow N will point from P to the center of the best-fitting circle or it will point in the opposite direction. If it points into the circle, we denote the curvature κ of the normal section at P by $1/r$; if it points away, by $-1/r$. Thus κ can be positive or negative, depending on the choice of the normal N. Negative κ means that the normal section is curving away from N, and positive means that it is curving toward N. Consequently this sign convention not only allows us to describe the amount of curviness of a normal section at the point P, but includes some directional information as well.

We are now ready to define a measure of curvature for a surface, our next major step. Two such measures of curvature are used by geometers today: the Gaussian curvature, and the mean curvature.

Let us consider all normal sections passing through a fixed point P of the surface. Then we can prove that there exist two special sections, C_1 and C_2, with curvatures κ_1 and κ_2, respectively, such that κ_1 is the largest and κ_2 the smallest curvature that a normal section at the point P can have.

Surfaces with different curvatures. The sign of K has a geometric meaning, whereas the sign of H depends on the choice of N.

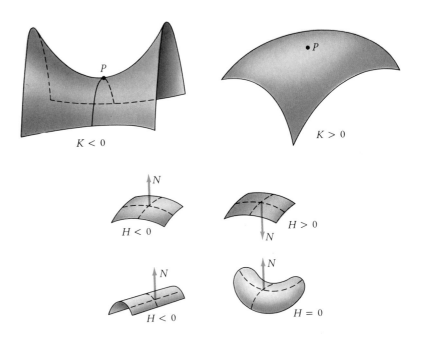

We now define the *Gaussian curvature K* of the surface at P as the product of the two principal curvatures κ_1 and κ_2,

$$K = \kappa_1 \cdot \kappa_2;$$

and we define the *mean curvature H* as the arithmetic average of the principal curvatures,

$$H = \frac{\kappa_1 + \kappa_2}{2}.$$

Now we can discuss the theorem of Lagrange in which he stated the minimal-surface equation.* This theorem will provide the geometric characterization of least-area surfaces that we are seeking:

At each regular point, a surface of minimal area must have a mean curvature of zero.

---

*The theorem as presented here was extended by Meusnier, one of the early differential geometers, in his *Mémoire sur la courbure des surfaces*, read to the French Academy in 1776 and published in 1785.

That is, the surfaces of minimal area satisfy the equation

$$H = 0.$$

(In the neighborhood of a regular point, a surface is smooth and looks like a slightly deformed disc.)

There is another physical interpretation of this equation. We can relate the pressure difference p between the sides of a soap film at any point to the mean curvature H of the film by the *Laplace equation*

$$p = TH,$$

where T denotes the surface tension of the liquid. The same equation relates the mean curvature of an interfacing surface between two liquids (or a liquid and a gas) to the difference in pressure between them.

Saying that the mean curvature must be zero is, therefore, equivalent to saying that we have the same pressure on both sides of a minimal surface. (In the interior of a soap bubble, however, we find higher pressure than outside of the bubble; thus a bubble is a *surface of constant mean curvature H* different from zero.)

It turns out that the surfaces that furnish an unstable equilibrium of area must likewise have a mean curvature of zero. For this reason it has become customary to use the term "minimal surface" for all surfaces having a mean curvature of zero, whether they minimize area or not. These are the objects that we shall now investigate.

From now on we shall refer to surfaces that are minimal for area (that is, for potential energy) as *stable minimal surfaces*, whereas the term *minimal surfaces* will indicate surfaces of zero mean curvature; such surfaces correspond to states of a soap film that are stationary relative to the potential energy of surface tension.

Stable minimal surfaces are those surfaces that, in principle, can be realized as soap films. However, the unstable minimal surfaces, the fleeting ghosts, are also interesting and important, even though the corresponding soap films cannot be produced. First, they are of interest to the mathematician as mathematical objects defined by a beautiful geometric condition. Second, they are needed to help us understand how minimal surfaces behave as we perturb their boundary contour.

What do minimal surfaces look like? If a surface has zero mean curvature at each point, then at each point it is curving both away and toward a given perpendicular direction. That is, *minimal surfaces either are flat or look like saddle surfaces.*

How Many Minimal Surfaces Can Span a Fixed Contour?

A natural question that we can ask about a given contour is *how many minimal surfaces can it bound.* Unfortunately, nearly nothing is known, even if we restrict ourselves to the much simpler question of *how many disc-type minimal surfaces can span a closed curve.* The figure in the margin on page 95 shows that there are certainly contours that can be spanned by more than one disc-type minimal surface, but are there contours that bound only one such surface?

A first answer has long been known: planar curves bound only one minimal surface, a planar one. A second result was found by Tibor Radó in 1932. He showed that, if a contour has a simple projection onto a convex curve in a plane, then it can bound only one disc-type minimal surface.

A curve with a convex simple projection onto a plane. A projection is simple if each of its points corresponds to only one point on the curve.

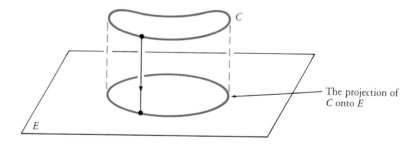

The projection of C onto E

The third and only other mathematical result on uniqueness uses the notion of *total curvature of a spatial curve.* This is a number that measures how much the entire contour curves. For example, a circle with radius 1 has a total curvature of 2π. If only a small part of a contour is very curvy, then the total curvature will not be too large. The following result is known: *If a given contour has a total curvature of less than 4π, then there can be only one disc-type minimal surface bounded by that contour.*

Thus one might hope to find at least an upper bound on the number of disc-type minimal surfaces that span a "not too complicated" contour. This hope has been completely dashed. It has recently been shown that, given any number N (say 100, 5000, 10^{100}, . . .) and any small positive number ϵ (say, $\frac{1}{10}$, $\frac{1}{8000}$, 10^{-200}, . . .), there exists a contour of total curvature less than $4\pi + \epsilon$ that bounds at least N disc-type minimal surfaces.

This striking theorem shows that, if the total curvature of a curve is even slightly larger than 4π, then very wild and quite unimaginable things can occur.

Except for the three uniqueness results that we just stated, nothing is known about the number of minimal surfaces or even about the number of disc-type minimal surfaces that span a given non-planar contour. There is no example of a curve that bounds more than one minimal surface and for which *all* minimal surfaces that span it (even of a specific genus) are known, nor are there even any examples that indicate plausible answers. For example, the figure below shows two minimal surfaces spanning the same uncomplicated contour, yet it is not known how many more minimal surfaces span this contour.

Two surfaces spanning the same contour.

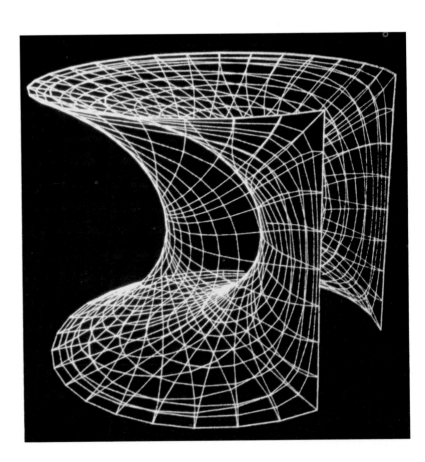

Even the apparently much simpler question, as to whether there are contours that bound infinitely many disc-type minimal surfaces, has not been answered. Intuition seems to tell us that a fixed contour will bound only finitely many such surfaces, but intuition can often be misleading in mathematics! There is, in fact, an intriguing curve that plausibly bounds infinitely many disc-type minimal surfaces, the monster curve depicted on page 99.

Let us see how this curve is constructed. First, take the contour in the upper figure shown below. This curve bounds at least two stable disc-type minimal surfaces (see the figure in the margin on page 95). Next, consider an infinite sequence C_1, C_2, C_3, . . . of curves of the same kind, selected in such a way that C_2 is half the size of C_1, curve C_3 half the size of C_2, and so on (see the middle figure below).

Join curves C_1 and C_2 by a small bridge, as shown in the lower figure, cutting some part of each curve to insure that a simple closed curve C^* is formed. Then we can join each of the two stable minimal

A simple closed curve that bounds at least two surfaces.

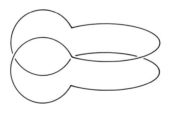

An infinite sequence C_1, C_2, C_3, . . . of contours of decreasing size (C_{i+1} is half the size of C_i) and tending to a point.

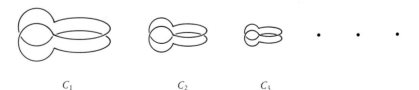

C_1 C_2 C_3

Two curves connected by a bridge.

C^*

Four surfaces that span the composite curve C^* in the illustration at the bottom of the preceding page.

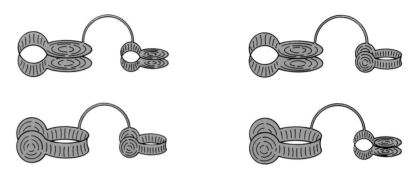

surfaces spanning curve C_1 to each of the two stable minimal surfaces spanning C_2 by adding a small ribbon spanning the bridge; so there are at least $2 \times 2 = 4$ combinations of disc-type surfaces bounded by C^*. Now it is plausible that, if the bridge is small enough, then, very close to each of the four "joint surfaces" generated by the bridging procedure, there exists a stable minimal surface.

In this way we have obtained from curves C_1 and C_2 a new simple closed curve that bounds four different stable minimal surfaces of the disc type. Why stop here? Attach to the contour C^* the third curve, C_3, in our sequence by a second bridge of half the size of the previous one. We then obtain another simple contour that, by the same plausibility argument as before, will bound at least $2 \times 2 \times 2 = 8$ stable minimal surfaces of the type of the disc. Next we attach C_3, C_4, C_5, and so on, by bridges of increasingly smaller size. By repeating this process indefinitely, we arrive at the simple closed curve C of finite length pictured on page 99. At each stage of the connecting procedure, we obtain at least twice as many minimal surfaces within the new contour as we had counted within the previous one. Thus we can argue that C bounds infinitely many disc-type minimal surfaces. Persuasive as this argument may seem, there is so far no complete mathematical proof for it. Still the monster curve might convince you that the situation could be worse than it appears to be at first sight.

On the other hand, the situation is not quite as bad as it may now seem. In fact, it has been proved in recent years that, if *one picks a simple smooth contour at random, the probability is zero that it bounds infinitely many disc-type minimal surfaces.* In other words, the "bad curves" are extremely rare; almost all smooth curves bound only a finite number of minimal surfaces of the type of the disc. This result does not contradict the statement that the monster curve bounds infinitely many minimal surfaces since it might belong to the set of bad curves. Moreover, the monster curve is not a smooth curve, even if we attached all bridges in a smooth way. The very tip of the tail of the monster curve is an extremely irregular point, a kind of kink.

For "very smooth" curves (the technical term is *analytic curves*) something more is known. Such a curve can bound only a finite number of least-area surfaces among all surfaces of the type of the disc.

The Algebraic Formula Relating the Minimal Surfaces That Span a Fixed Contour

Despite all the peculiarities discussed in the preceding section, a way has recently been discovered to relate *all* possible disc-type minimal surfaces bounded by a fixed wire. To explain this result, let us return to our simple model of the deformed steel bowl situated over a plane as shown in the margin on page 104. If, for this bowl, we consider the height h above the plane, then there are three equilibrium points for h, the two minima P_1 and P_2 and one unstable equilibrium point P_3. Imagine a spider walking along the inside of this bowl. If the spider starts at either P_1 or P_2, then its height above the plane will increase regardless of the direction in which it walks. However, at P_3 the situation is different. There the spider can choose a direction along which its height above the plane decreases. Like our skier in Chapter 4, the spider is decreasing its potential energy. Let us give a name to the maximal number of mutually perpendicular directions in which the spider can walk away from an equilibrium point and yet decrease its height; we will call it the *characteristic number* of the equilibrium point. For P_1 and P_2 the characteristic number is 0; for P_3 it is 1.

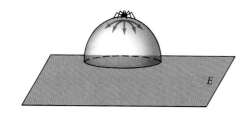

A spider on an upside-down bowl.

The upper figure at the left shows an upside-down bowl over a plane E. The only equilibrium point is P, the top of the inverted bowl. Whatever direction the spider crawls from P reduces its height; so the characteristic number of P is 2.

Let us return to our first bowl, where we have the three equilibrium points with characteristic numbers $\lambda_1 = 0$, $\lambda_2 = 0$, $\lambda_3 = 1$. We then form the sum

$$(-1)^{\lambda_1} + (-1)^{\lambda_2} + (-1)^{\lambda_3} = 1 + 1 - 1 = 1.$$

Now suppose we take *any* hemispherical bowl and deform it (but not along its border), creating in this way some number of pits, passes, or peaks, say, n equilibrium points $P_1, \ldots, P_n$ with characteristic numbers $\lambda_1, \ldots, \lambda_n$ (see the lower figure at the left).

A valley with three pits.

A polyhedron that can be inscribed in a sphere.

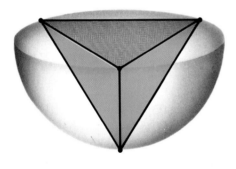

An inverted baseless pyramid in a bowl.

The reader may check that all these examples will satisfy the remarkable equation

$$(-1)^{\lambda_1} + (-1)^{\lambda_2} + \cdots + (-1)^{\lambda_n} = 1.$$

This equation, called *Morse's equation,* is forced upon us by some mathematical structure hidden within the topological nature of the bowl. The key to understanding this structure is a discovery made by Leonhard Euler. He noticed that, if a polyhedron is inscribed in a sphere, then

$$V - E + F = 2,$$

where V is the number of vertices of the polyhedron, E the number of edges, and F the number of faces. This is true for any inscribed polyhedron and thus must belong to the topological nature of the sphere.

Something similar holds for the hemisphere, our open undeformed bowl (which topologically is a sphere with one hole). Inscribe any polyhedron inside of this bowl, keeping in mind that it is open at the top. For simplicity, let us take an inverted three-sided pyramid that is missing its base (corresponding to the open top of the bowl). Here we have $V = 4$, $E = 6$, $F = 3$, and therefore

$$V - E + F = 1.$$

The same number was obtained in counting the equilibrium points and their characteristic numbers in Morse's equation. Moreover, we have $V - E + F = 1$ for any such inscribed polyhedron. The equality between the sums,

$$(-1)^{\lambda_1} + (-1)^{\lambda_2} + \cdots + (-1)^{\lambda_n} = V - E + F,$$

is a profound fact discovered by the mathematician Marston Morse about fifty years ago (and is the basis of what is now called Morse theory). It is particularly striking because it connects the concept of equilibria in the calculus of variations with concepts in topology (the theory of form and shape of surfaces), and this mixture is essential to its proof.

But what does all this have to do with minimal surfaces? By the finiteness theorem we mentioned in the preceding section, almost all contours behave "reasonably" in the sense that they bound only a finite number of disc-type minimal surfaces. Let C be any such reasonable curve. Then, for some integer N, there are exactly N disc-type minimal surfaces spanning C. We shall label them $S_1, S_2, \ldots, S_N$. Only some of these may actually be minima for area.

There is a theorem requiring a great deal of mathematical development that assigns to each of these minimal surfaces S_i a characteristic number λ_i analogous in meaning to the characteristic numbers in our bowl model. In particular, if S_i is of minimum area, then $\lambda_i = 0$. By combining ideas from the fields of topology and the calculus of variations, it can be proved that Morse's equation holds:

$$(-1)^{\lambda_1} + (-1)^{\lambda_2} + \cdots + (-1)^{\lambda_N} = 1.$$

This equation provides a new proof of the previously mentioned result that the existence of two minima implies the existence of a third, unstable minimal surface (see the illustration at the bottom of page 104). Suppose that we had two surfaces of minimum area spanning a reasonable contour and no other minimal surface. Then, because the characteristic number of each minimum is zero, the left side of Morse's equation would read

$$(-1)^{\lambda_1} + (-1)^{\lambda_2} = (-1)^0 + (-1)^0 = 1 + 1 = 2 \neq 1,$$

a violation of Morse's equality. So there must be another minimal surface with an odd characteristic number. Thus this other surface could not be a local minimum and would have to be unstable. In general, by Morse's equation, the existence of n minimal surfaces of minimum area that span a contour implies that there must be another $n - 1$ unstable minimal surfaces bounded by the same contour.

Catenoid and Helicoid

In the preceding sections we considered minimal surfaces bounded by a single closed curve. Let us now investigate minimal surfaces with two or more boundary curves. Such surfaces that have minimum area correspond to soap films bounded by several wires.

What will happen if we dip two closed wires into a soap solution and then withdraw them? We may obtain two separate soap films, one within each wire, or, if we are lucky, we might see *one connected soap film* bounded by both wires, like those shown at the left. The connected soap films pictured here are of the same topological type as an annulus, which, in turn, is of the same topological type as a sphere with two holes (see the upper figure on page 98). If you try the experi-

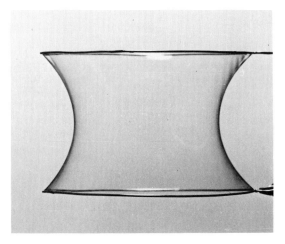

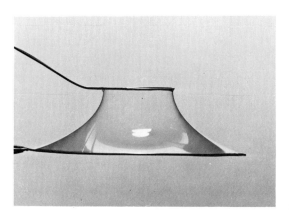

A soap film spanning two circular wires: (top) same size circles; (bottom) different size circles.

A system of three minimal surfaces with two boundary circles.

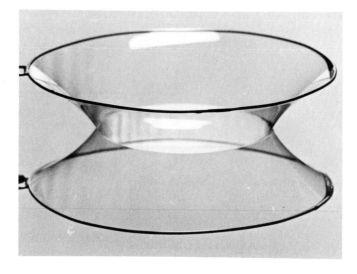

ment yourself, you may find it impossible to obtain these surfaces if the wires are too far apart; even if they are close to each other, you may not get a smooth connected soap film, but instead a system of three minimal surfaces, as is shown above. Such systems of soap films were not on our list of mathematical surfaces that might span a boundary contour; we are once again forced to extend our definition of a surface. In stable equilibria, systems of soap films have the property that only three surfaces can meet at a liquid edge, and they must intersect at angles of 120°. We shall discuss this phenomenon at greater length in the next section.

The system of three soap films spanning two wires is a relative minimum of area, but it has larger area than the smooth connected annular (ring-shaped) film. It is a simple trick to force the annular surface, and not the system, to be formed in the soap-film experiment. Place a stick (or a finger) through the wires before withdrawing them from the soap solution; then the annular surface will appear when the wires are withdrawn.

There is an amazing relation between this annular region and a well-known mechanical curve. Let us consider surfaces of revolution. One of the simplest ways to produce a surface is to revolve a curve about a fixed axis. Are there any minimal surfaces that are surfaces of revolution? One candidate is obvious: the plane. It can be obtained by rotating a straight line L about an axis that meets L perpendicularly.

Are there other surfaces of revolution with vanishing mean curvature besides the obvious planar surfaces, plane and disc? There is exactly one other type, and this is how it can be generated. Just hang a

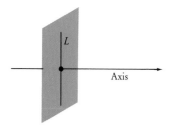

The plane as a surface of revolution.

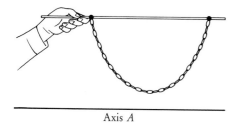

Axis A

A horizontal stick with a chain.

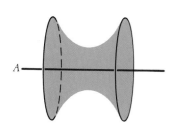

A catenoid as a surface of revolution.

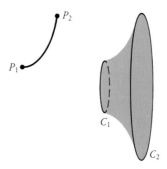

A catenoid bounded by two circles with different radii.

chain at both ends from a stick. When it is in rest, you have produced the catenary. By revolving it about an axis that is parallel to the stick and below the chain, you will obtain the only kind of nonplanar minimal surface that is a surface of revolution, provided that the lowest point of the catenary is at height $h = \sqrt{b^2 - l^2}$ above the axis of rotation. Here l denotes half of the length of the chain, and b is the distance between the stick and the axis of rotation. This minimal surface, which is *the only curved minimal surface of revolution,* was discovered by Euler in 1744. For obvious reasons it has been christened the *catenoid.* As can be seen below, a catenoid can be bounded by circles of different radii.

We have already mentioned that no connected minimal surface will form if the two circles are too far apart. What happens if we start with a catenoid and move the two boundary circles C_1 and C_2 apart? If you perform the corresponding experiment with a soap film, you will find that, at a critical distance between the two coaxial wires C_1 and C_2, the film will break and jump into two discs spanning C_1 and C_2 separately. The distance at which the catenoid must break is known precisely. If, for instance, the circular wires C_1 and C_2 have the same radius R, the critical distance d is about 1.325487 times R.

In fact, the two circles bound two catenoids provided that their distance is less than the critical number d, but only one is stable (the unstable one bends in more), so only one connected soap film can be held by the two circular wires. The other stable configuration is the pair of discs spanning C_1 and C_2. Thus we see again that the existence of two stable soap films implies that of a third, an unstable one.

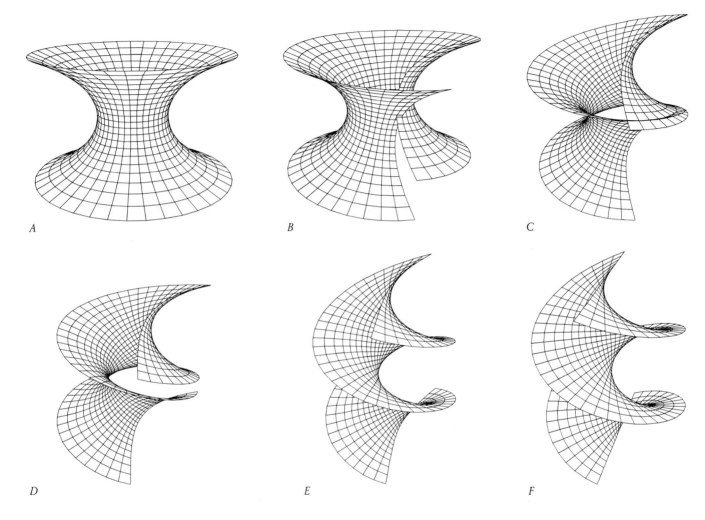

A

B

C

D

E

F

Isometric deformation of catenoid into
helicoid.

With the catenoid we can carry out a very curious experiment. First we build a model of this surface out of some plastic material. We then cut the model along one of its meridians and pull the two cut ends gently apart, thereby twisting the surface, as shown above. In this way we are able to bend the catenoid without any distortion into a piece of another celebrated minimal surface, the *helicoid*. The isometric deformation or bending of the catenoid into the helicoid we have described is even more remarkable because it can be carried out in such a way that all the intermediate surfaces during the bending procedure are minimal surfaces too!

After the catenoid, the helicoid, or screw surface, is the second oldest example of a curved minimal surface. It was already well known in 1776, when the French geometer Meusnier discovered that it had zero mean curvature. In fact, architects used parts of the helicoid to build winding staircases, remarkable examples of which can be found in some of the great European residences.

The construction principle of the helicoid is fairly easy to understand. One takes a straight line L that meets some fixed axis A perpendicularly. Then one turns L with constant speed around A and, at the same time, the intersection point P of L with A moves with constant speed along A. The superposition of these two motions results in a screw motion of the line L, and the surface swept out by L is a helicoid. The middle figure below shows the part of the helicoid lying inside a cylinder with axis A. The helicoid intersects such a cylinder in two helices, or screw lines, C_1 and C_2, that together form a double helix. Imagine now that each curve is replaced by a thin strip of paper, as in the lower right-hand figure. Then we obtain a geometric figure that serves as a model for the DNA molecule, the carrier of the genetic code.

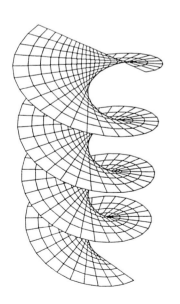

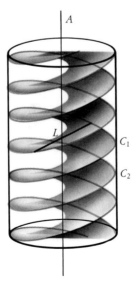

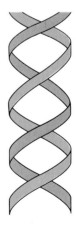

A helicoid, which can be used in the design of winding staircases.

The generation of a helicoid.

Double helix.

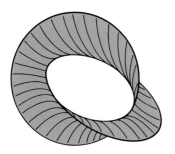

A minimal surface spanning two interlocking curves.

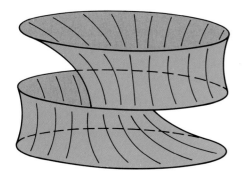

One of infinitely many minimal surfaces that spans a contour consisting of three coaxial circles.

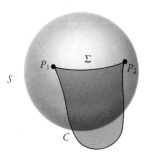

A minimal surface with a partially free boundary.

The catenoid is the simplest example of a minimal surface bounded by a configuration consisting of more than one closed curve. Another example is depicted in the upper figure at the left, where the minimal surface spans two interlocking wires. A system of wires also provides an example of a boundary configuration that can be spanned by infinitely many minimal surfaces of the same topological type. (This, as you may recall, is one of the central questions in the study of minimal surfaces.) Choose as a boundary a set of three coaxial circular wires of equal radius and of small but equal distance. Then we can show that there is an infinite family of minimal surfaces of genus zero bounded by these wires. A picture of one such surface is given in the middle figure at the left. All of the members of the family are obtained by simple rotation of one of them about the axis of the circles. Thus one might argue that this is not a real counterexample to finiteness. This objection is somewhat justified; so we might call two surfaces "really different" if we cannot generate one from the other by a motion of space. The question of how many "really different" minimal surfaces of the same topological type can span a given configuration of 1, 2, 3, . . ., curves is completely open.

Liquid Edges, and the Three Fundamental Angles of 90°, 120°, and 109°28'16"

Consider the soap film pictured in the lower figure at the left. This stable minimal surface differs from those we have already encountered. Its boundary does not lie entirely on a given wire, but lies partially on a prescribed surface (called a *supporting surface*). Hence the boundary of such a soap film is not, as in the Plateau problem, completely prescribed, but can choose an optimal position on the supporting surface.

To generate this example, we have taken a surface S, made of glass or plexiglass, to which a curve C, a wire, is attached at two points P_1 and P_2. The framework $\langle C,S \rangle$, consisting of the surface S and the attached wire C, is then dipped into a soap solution. When we withdraw it, a soap film attached to the wire C will form; yet some part of its boundary will be a liquid edge on the supporting surface S. This liquid edge, which we call Σ, is generated by the soap film in such a way that area is minimized. The curve Σ is said to be the *free boundary* of the soap film (or of the stable minimal surface) on the supporting surface S. The upper figure on the next page shows soap films the entire boundary of each of which is a free boundary on the surface S.

Minimal surfaces with totally free boundaries.

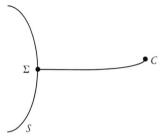

Right angles at the free boundary (a cross-sectional view).

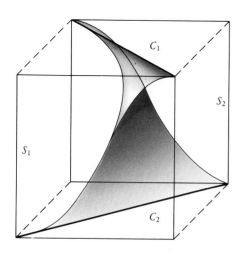

Gergonne's surface.

We cannot say very much about the shape of the free boundary Σ. In fact, nearly every curve on S can be part of the free boundary of a soap film. Yet one law can be verified in all experiments: smooth parts of a soap film will intersect a smooth supporting surface perpendicularly, as indicated in the middle figure at the left.

H. A. Schwarz gave a rigorous mathematical proof of this fact for minimal surfaces that Plateau had experimentally observed for soap films. Thus we have:

RULE 1. If a minimal surface has a free boundary Σ on a surface of support S, then it meets S along the curve Σ at a right angle.

This is the 90° rule, which we will meet again and again.[*]

The oldest problem on minimal surfaces with a free boundary was posed by the French mathematician J. D. Gergonne in 1816:

Divide a cube by a surface M (shown in gray in the lower illustration at the left) in two parts in such a way that M is attached at two inverse diagonals C_1 and C_2 that lie on opposite faces of the cube, and M is of minimal area.

The first attempts to answer this question were in error, and the solution was only found by Schwarz in 1872. This minimal surface, though found by Schwarz, is usually called *Gergonne's surface*. It is attached to two other faces S_1 and S_2 of the cube at a right angle.

Moreover, Schwarz found infinitely many surfaces of zero mean curvature bounded by the frame $\langle C_1, C_2, S_1, S_2 \rangle$ that intersect S_1 and S_2 perpendicularly and are "really different," that is, not congruent, although only one of them has least area. Hence this boundary-value problem has "really" infinitely many solutions.

Another boundary configuration $\langle C_1, C_2, S \rangle$ with infinitely many "really different" solutions, formed by helicoids (winding staircases), can be obtained from a cylinder surface S and two perpendicular straight lines C_1 and C_2 that pass through the cylinder axis at different heights.

---

[*] The existence theory for minimal surfaces with free boundaries was begun by Richard Courant in 1940, and in 1951 Hans Lewy carried out the first detailed study of the free boundary Σ. However, Schwarz and the Finnish mathematicians Neovius, Stenius, and Tallqvist had already proved the existence of minimal surfaces that span a configuration $<C, S>$ for the case where S was a plane and C was a polygon with endpoints on this plane.

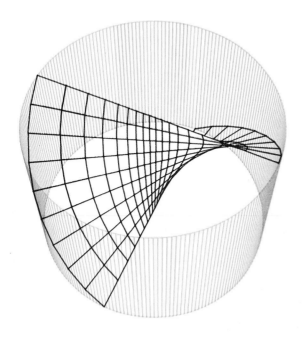

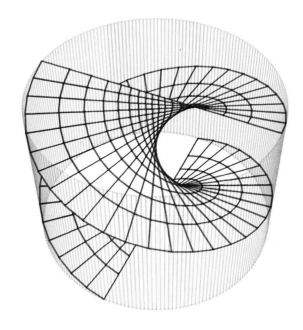

Three of infinitely many "really different" minimal surfaces that span a certain boundary configuration.

Courant had noticed that we can obtain soap films (that is, minima of area) that span a given frame ⟨C,S⟩ and that are really different and are even of different topological type (see the figure below).

Minimal surfaces with partially free boundary and of different topological type within the same boundary configuration ⟨C,S⟩.

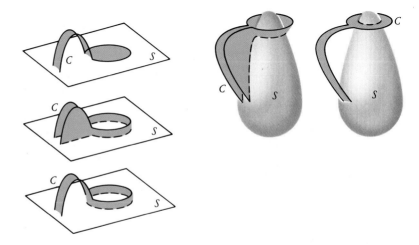

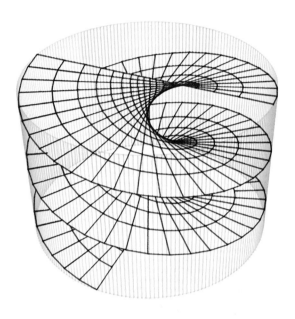

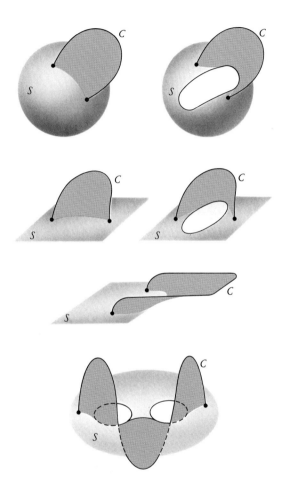

The obstacle problem with (partially) free boundaries.

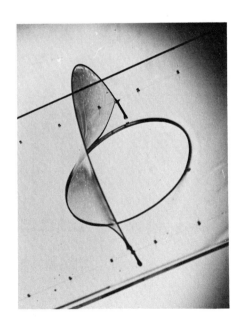

A free boundary attaches tangentially to the boundary of the supporting surface.

A new situation arises if the supporting surface S itself has some boundary, and if the soap film is attached at least in part to the boundary. Then Rule 1 is no longer correct, because the soap film is now not completely free to move; the boundary of S forms an obstacle. But the soap film will still meet the "interior part" of the supporting surface S at a right angle. It is interesting to note that, in general, the free boundary of a soap film will attach tangentially to the boundary of S. This has been verified by experiment (see the photograph on the left) and by rigorous mathematical proof.

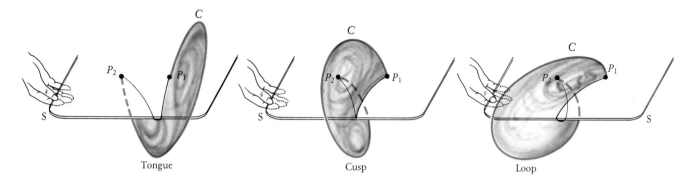

The three configurations—tongue, cusp, loop—that a soap film can form within a configuration consisting of a plate and a wire led around a plate.

Soap-film experiments showing tongue, cusp, and loop.

However, the free boundary Σ may in some very special cases have a singularity, in the form of a cusp. This can be generated in the following way. Take a glass plate S; fix a wire C at some point P_1 on the upper side of S, lead C around past the edge of S, and then fix it at some point P_2 on the lower side of S (see the figure above). As long as C looks like a circle cut at one point and the two loose ends are moved only slightly apart, the soap film formed has the shape of a "tongue." If, however, the wire C is deformed in the right manner, the tongue will change into a loop. By carrying out this experiment very carefully, you will obtain the cusp as an intermediate position of the wire. The photographs below show the three stages.

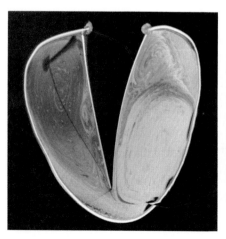
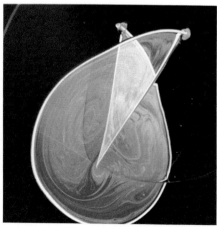

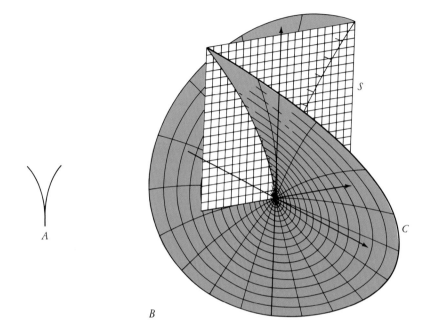

A

B

Furthermore, part *B* of the figure above depicts a frame, consisting of a half-plane *S* and a curve *C*, that bounds a minimal surface the free boundary of which has a cusp. This surface, which can be modeled by a soap film, was discovered by Henneberg in 1876. Its free boundary is a curve called the *Neil parabola* or *semicubical parabola* (part *A*). Its two branches can be described by $y = x^{3/2}$ and $y = -x^{3/2}$, whereas an ordinary parabola is given by $y = x^2$.

Free boundaries on supporting surfaces *S* are not the only situations in which we can have liquid edges of soap films. Several soap films within a frame can meet at one or more edges to form a stable arrangement of films, that is, a system of surfaces that minimizes area within a given boundary configuration. For example, three arcs C_1, C_2, C_3 meeting in two points (see the figure below) can be spanned by a

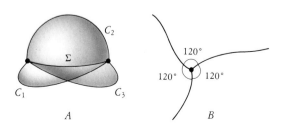

A

B

Soap-film system.

system of soap films with a common liquid edge Σ at which each pair of the three films forms an angle of 120°.

Another example is provided by a tetrahedral frame (see the photograph on the next page). It bounds a system of six soap films with four liquid edges. Again, any two films meeting along the same edge must meet at an angle of 120°. Moreover, the four liquid edges have exactly one vertex in common, and each pair of edges meets at an angle ϕ of 109°28'16"; to be precise, ϕ is the angle having a cosine of $-\frac{1}{3}$.

Plateau discovered by experiments that these two examples are typical, and nothing else can happen. Thus we have the second rule for a stable configuration of soap films:

> RULE 2. Three smooth minimal surfaces of an area-minimizing system of surfaces intersect in a smooth line at an angle of 120°. Only four such lines, each formed by the intersection of three surfaces, can intersect at a single point. At such a point, the angle between any two adjacent lines is 109°28'16".

A rigorous mathematical proof of the part of this rule concerning the 120° has been known for a long time and is rather easy to obtain, provided that the lines of intersection are already known to be smooth. However, a satisfactory proof of the second part was given only recently.

The main concept used to prove the second part of Rule 2 is the following. Suppose that the minimal surfaces and their lines of inter-

Soap films in tetrahedron.

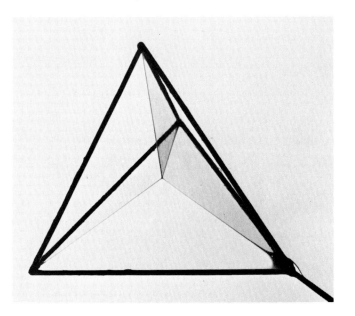

section are known to be smooth curves. Then we pick some point P from the system of surfaces, and magnify smaller and smaller neighborhoods of P to the same size. Thus, in the limit, all surfaces look flat and all lines seem to be straight. The area-minimizing property of the original system of surfaces implies that the new configuration of the flat surfaces obtained by magnification is also area-minimizing. Now we draw a sphere centered at P, and let it intersect the flat configuration of surfaces. The intersecting lines are great circles. The area-minimizing property of the flat system means that no more than three of these great circles can meet at a vertex, where they must enclose an angle of 120°; otherwise the area of the configuration could be reduced.

So the next question is, what are all the possible networks of great circles on the sphere that meet three at a time at equal angles of 120°? To answer this, we must solve Steiner's problem on the sphere instead of in the plane. Using spherical trigonometry, we can show that only ten such geodesic networks are possible, and a more detailed analysis shows that only three of the ten are area-minimizing. These are the first three (parts A, B, and C) in the catalogue of ten depicted on the next two pages. The first one corresponds to a flat surface, and the second two to the systems depicted in the lower figure on page 125 and in the figure at the top of this page. This proves Rule 2.

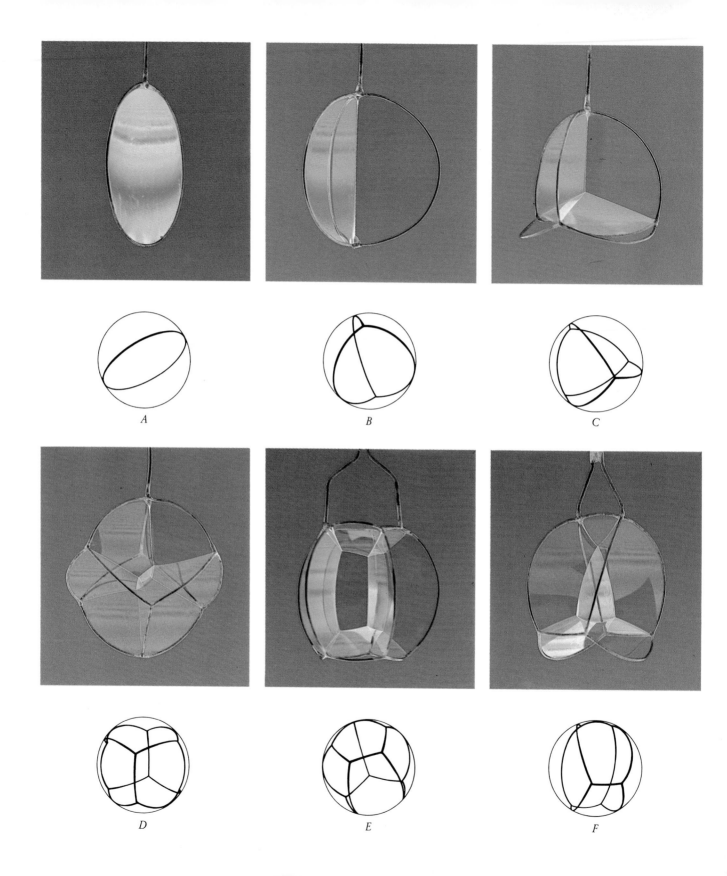

A

B

C

D

E

F

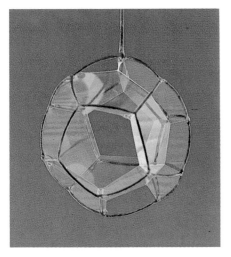

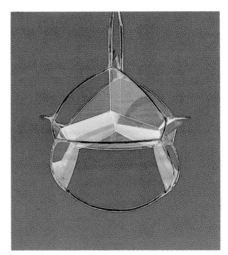

G

H

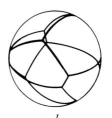
I

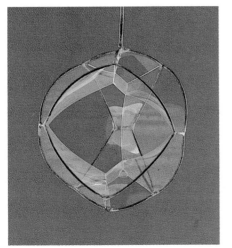

There are ten possible networks of great circles on a sphere meeting three at a time at angles of 120°. They are shown here in diagrams A through J. The soap films that span diagrams A, B, and C agree with the surface systems obtained by the "magnification procedure," whereas the soap-film systems in diagrams D through J are different from the corresponding "magnified objects," called "cones," which are generated by all the straight arcs drawn from the center of the sphere to the points on the spherical network. These observations yield a "physical proof" of the fact that the cones for diagrams A, B, and C are area-minimizing, whereas the cones

for D through J are not. There is also a rigorous mathematical proof of this fact.

The ten networks A through J can briefly be described as follows: diagram A is a great circle; B is three halves of great circles; C is a spherical tetrahedron; D is a spherical hexahedron; E is a spherical prism with a pentagon as base; F is a spherical prism over a triangle; G is a spherical dodecahedron; H consists of two quadrangles and eight congruent pentagons; I consists of four congruent quadrangles and four congruent pentagons; and J consists of three quadrangles and six pentagons.

J

The systems of soap films that span polyhedral frames form very beautiful configurations of surfaces. A frame can bound several different configurations of soap films, even several "really different" ones. A very striking example of this phenomenon results from using an octahedral frame. The different soap-film configurations that span this frame can be generated by withdrawing the wire framework from the soap solution in different ways; some experimenting is needed.

Soap film in an octahedron.

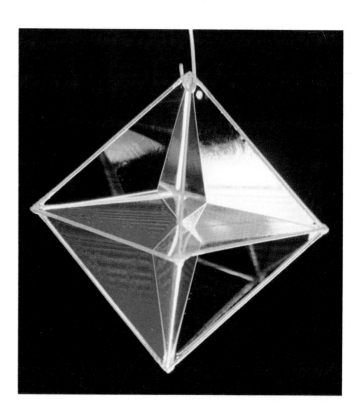

One soap-film configuration can often be changed into a different one by gently blowing at the surfaces; but sometimes shaking the frame may work as well.

An interesting combination of the 90° and 120° principles can be used to solve Steiner's general problem experimentally by means of soap films. In this problem we are given n points, and then must look for a network of lines that connects all the given points and has the smallest possible total length.

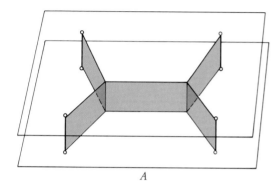

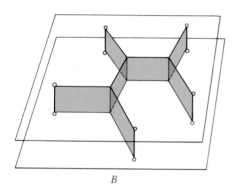

Soap-film solution of Steiner's problem for (A) four points and (B) five points.

Suppose we make a frame consisting of two parallel glass or clear plastic plates; these are connected by n parallel pins of the same size that meet both plates perpendicularly. If this framework is immersed in a soap solution and withdrawn, a system of planar soap films is formed. These films are attached to the pins, and they have two kinds of liquid edges, both of which are straight lines. One type adheres to the glass (or plastic), which it meets at 90° because these liquid edges are free boundaries on a supporting surface. The other type is where three films meet forming three angles of 120° (see the figures on the left). Suppose we now mark the position of n given points on one of the plates, and then fix the pins at these marks. Then the subsystem of liquid edges on either plate will provide an experimental solution of the given Steiner problem, for these edges are subject to the same rules as the Steiner solutions. Moreover, the total area of the soap-film system obviously equals the distance of the two plates times the total length of the liquid edges that lie on one of the plates. Since the soap-film system minimizes area, the subsystem of edges on one plate must minimize length among all connections between the n given points.

Periodic Minimal Surfaces

H. A. Schwarz was the first to solve Plateau's problem for the simplest nonplanar contour C. He chose C to be a quadrilateral, a circuit around four of the six edges of a regular tetrahedron. Schwarz announced his results in 1865, and he also presented three models he had constructed. The frameworks of these models were made of thin wire, and the spanning minimal surfaces consisted of a skin of gelatine. The first model is shown in the figure on the next page.*

Schwarz had discovered that soap films with a free boundary on a surface S must meet S perpendicularly. This led him to consider the following problem. Suppose that $\langle C_1, \ldots, C_k, S_1, \ldots, S_l \rangle$ is a connected array of k straight lines $C_1, \ldots, C_k$ and of l planar surfaces $S_1, \ldots, S_l$, a *Schwarz chain*. This determines a minimal surface that has a boundary on the chain and that intersects the surfaces $S_1, \ldots, S_l$ along its liquid edges at an angle of 90°. Problems of this kind could be

---

* The paper describing this work was presented to the Berlin Academy in 1867 and was awarded the academy's prize. Schwarz's paper is still one of the marvels of mathematical literature. Even a modern reader may enjoy it because of its beautiful style and its flawless presentation. Bernhard Riemann had solved the problem in 1861/62 but did not publish his results. It was his student Hattendorff who revised Riemann's manuscript in 1866 and published it posthumously in 1867.

Schwarz's surface in an equilateral frame.
Here we have a connected array of four
straight lines bounding this minimal surface.

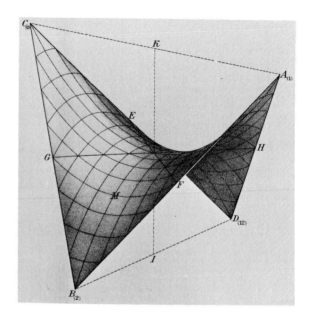

explicitly solved in Schwarz's time. Moreover, Schwarz discovered two important *reflection principles for minimal surfaces:* reflection of a minimal surface across a straight line and reflection across a plane. Both reflection principles allow us to build up "large" minimal surfaces from small pieces. These reflection principles can be formulated as follows.

RULE 3. If a part of the boundary of a minimal surface M is contained in a straight line, then its reflection M^* across the line is also a minimal surface, and the union of M and M^* forms a smooth minimal surface as well.

RULE 4. If a minimal surface M meets a plane at a right angle, then its mirror image M^* at the plane is a minimal surface that, together with M, forms an extended surface that is a smooth minimal surface.

Consider now a minimal surface M whose boundary consists of several pieces that lie either on straight lines or on planes that meet M perpendicularly. Then we can reflect M across each straight piece of the boundary, and we can also form all the mirror images of M across those planes that are struck by M at a right angle. In this way we get a new surface; it consists of the original surface M, the *basic unit*, and of its reflections and mirror images, which we generated by employing the reflections described in Rules 3 and 4. The new surface is a smooth minimal surface, and its boundary (like that of all reflections and mirror images of the basic unit *M*) has the same properties as the boundary of *M*. That is, its boundary consists of finitely many pieces that lie either on straight lines or on planes that meet the surface at right angles. We therefore can proceed with the process of extension: each reflection and mirror image of the basic unit can be considered to be a new basic unit to which the two reflection rules may be applied.

The extension process will terminate if at some stage no boundary is left at which a reflection can be carried out. For instance, if the basic unit is a half-plane, only one reflection is possible. We can, however, prove that *for a finite basic unit the extension process will never come to an end.*

We therefore can expect to arrive at an "infinitely extended" minimal surface. We must, however, anticipate that this surface will in general have *self-intersections.* Only very special Schwarzian chains bound minimal surfaces that, considered to be basic units, lead to an *infinitely extended minimal surface without self-intersections;* such an object is called a *periodic minimal surface.*

As early as 1867, Schwarz pointed out that the (uniquely determined) minimal surface spanning the quadrilateral in the figure below is the basic unit of a periodic minimal surface. The top left photograph on the next page depicts part of this periodic surface. The model was made by the American physicist Alan H. Schoen in 1968/69.

Parts of the Schwarz periodic surface.

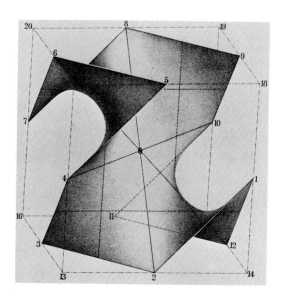

Upper left: A model produced by Alan Schoen of Schwarz's periodic minimal surface based on the quadrilateral.

Upper right and lower left and right: Models produced by Alan Schoen of Schwarz's second periodic minimal surface.

Schwarz and other authors found additional periodic minimal surfaces, some of which are represented in the photographs above and on the facing page.

Periodic minimal surfaces and related structures might be interesting for biologists, who have noticed that separating walls between organic and inorganic material in the skeletons of echinoderms (starfish, sea urchins, and related creatures) resemble certain kinds of periodic minimal surfaces.

Left: A model of a periodic minimal surface discovered by the Finnish mathematician Neovius and produced by Alan Schoen.
Right: A model of Schoen's surface ("gyroid") produced by Alan Schoen.

Minimal Surfaces as Roofs and Tents

In the past thirty years, the elegant constructions of the architect Frei Otto and his collaborators have justifiably become well known. Their buildings are not constructions in the classical sense of architecture but are more like an arrangement of tents. For instance, the German Pavilion at the 1967 World Exposition in Montreal, designed by Frei Otto and Rolf Gutbrod, resembled an unearthly landscape formed by a single membrane of varying height. Its contours were supported at the high points by masts, and at the low points the membrane was anchored to the ground. The prestressed membrane, consisting of a transparent material, was supported by a steel wire net, which was connected to the mast heads and anchor points by a system of edge ropes, ridges, and eye loops. The "eye loops" (the importance of which we shall explain later) were filled with clear plastic.

Roof of the Olympic Stadium (Munich, 1972).

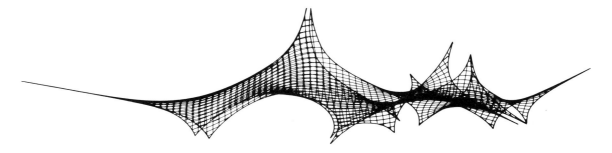

Interior view of the Olympic Stadium.

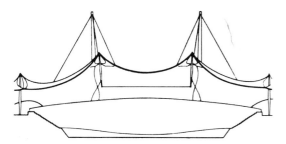

Roof for the Olympic Athletic Arena (Munich, 1972) showing five main units of minimal surfaces, eight eye units, two suspension points, two central secondary points, eight support points, and twenty-nine anchor points. Maximum span, 443 feet; maximum height, 180 feet.

Another celebrated design is the roof of the Olympic Stadium in Munich. This is also a tentlike construction formed by saddle-type nets with two suspension points, two support masts, various anchor points, and a single frontal-edge cable 1,443 feet in length. The net is covered by a translucent acrylic sheeting. The steel masts are 190 feet, and the roof has a maximal span of 213 feet. The roofs of the Olympic

Exterior view of the Olympic Athletic Arena.

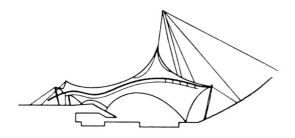

Roof for the Olympic Swimming Arena (Munich, 1972) showing a minimal surface with one suspension point and thirteen stabilization and anchor points. Maximum span, 279 feet; maximum height, 164 feet.

Exterior view of the Olympic Swimming Arena.

Athletic Arena and of the Olympic Swimming Arena are two other constructions of the same type.

The similarity between tents and the roofs of Frei Otto is not an accident; they have several principles of construction in common. First, both are conceived as light-weight structures, designed to be economical by using the least possible amount of construction material. Second, they are designed to be easily erected, dismantled, and transported. Third, the principal force acting on these roofs is *tensile stress;* only a few parts, such as the masts or supporting arches, are exposed to *compression.*

Tents and lightweight roofs thus differ in an essential way from most conventional buildings, in which the amount of material used is generally out of proportion to the actual load requirements of the building. Ordinary buildings cannot be moved to other locations without great difficulty. Moreover most of the materials used in them, such as stone or bricks, can be subjected to compression forces, but not to stress. The bending and buckling forces in these buildings are usually dealt with by using a large amount of extra material, leading to inevitable waste and unnecessary cost.

As we have already seen, nature provides a handy device for detecting optimal shapes of surfaces within a given contour: just permit a soap film to span a desired boundary configuration. If it does not easily break, it will be in stable equilibrium; it is a minimal surface that minimizes area. Frei Otto and his collaborators have used soap films as a principal tool for their architectural designs. They have carried out many experiments to find elegant forms that can be transformed into real buildings. Most of these experiments were in principle already known to Plateau and other researchers, but Frei Otto's ingenious variations of the geometric design of the supporting boundaries of the soap films led to marvelous new forms that had not been conceived before.

One type of material used by Frei Otto in these experiments is hair-thin thread tied to the ends of needles or thin sticks, which in turn are fastened to holes in a plexiglass plate (see the photograph below). If you dip such a configuration into a soap solution and then withdraw it, the soap film will pull the threads taut in order to achieve a position of minimal area. By fixing the threads to needles of different height, you can obtain a spectacular tentlike shape.

For these soap-film models to be transformed into architectural forms, they must be carefully photographed and measured. Solid models are then produced and tested in wind-tunnels. Special measuring devices inform the experimenters about the stress that might occur under the impact of wind and snow. Then, in the actual construction, thin, high-strength steel cables replace the hair-thin thread used in the soap-film models; the membranes are usually made out of synthetic material.

A soap film bounded by a system of threads.

Thread on a disclike minimal surface:
(A) loose thread; (B) thread tightened.

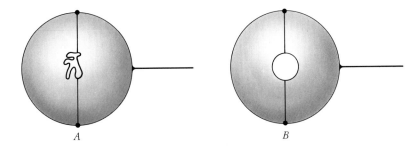

A

B

Very interesting aesthetic effects can be achieved by the following procedure, which you can easily carry out yourself. Take a wire in the form of a planar curve, attach a handle to it, and dip it in a soap solution and then remove it to form a (planar) soap film. Then place a thin loop of thread onto the film, where it will lie crumbled and without tension. With a blunt instrument and some delicacy, you will be able to break the soap within the loop without destroying the film outside the loop. The soap film wants to reduce its area; so it pulls the thread tight, into the shape of a circle (see the figures above). A circle formed in this way is shown below. Here the thread is not attached by strings to the exterior curve as shown above, but one of its points P is tied to a needle, which is fastened to the ground. If we lower the needle, as in the photograph on the next page, the thread is pulled out of its planar position and becomes a spatial curve, which, incidently,

A planar minimal surface bounded by a circular thread.

A thread under vertical stress (pulled down-ward).

will be a very smooth curve of constant curvature, except for the point *P* and any parts of the loop that cling together. The soap film bounded by its exterior contour and the "eye loop" is now a nonplanar surface, and its curviness will provide a stable form for possible later architectural use. For example, the photographs on the facing page show how Frei Otto's institute in Stuttgart was conceived. In the model, an exterior contour was formed by threads tied to needles that are inserted into a plate. Moreover, a gallowslike upper needle supported a loop to which the soap film was attached. In the building, steel cables have replaced the threads, and the interior of the loop has been filled with a clear plastic material, which, together with the windows on the ground floor, floods the interior with light during daytime.

You can now easily understand the principles of design and construction that Frei Otto used on the roof of the Olympic Stadium in Munich and on the German Pavilion in Montreal. Here we find a whole system of supporting masts (instead of a single gallows) and, accordingly, many eye loops. The results are tentlike roofs of great elegance. In addition to the supporting eye loops, other supporting elements, such as ridges, humps, or ropes, are also used (see the figures on page 142).

It is well known and easily verified that you can push a soap film with a blunt object such as your finger, but not with a needle, which will pierce the film. On the other hand, using the edge of a sharp knife, or a very thin thread, you can lift a soap film. This raises the questions of what objects can be used to lift a soap film, and exactly what a "*set*

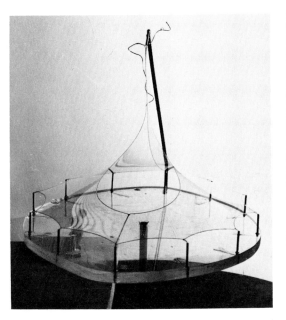

The Institute for Lightweight Structures, Stuttgart: (upper left) model; (upper right) network; (right) the finished building.

Structural elements of lightweight buildings.

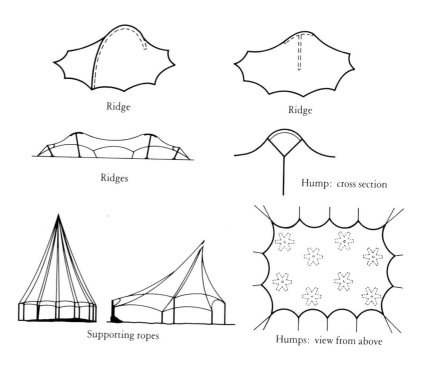

Ridge   Ridge

Ridges   Hump: cross section

Supporting ropes   Humps: view from above

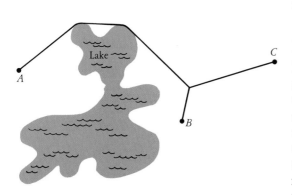

Generalization of Steiner's problem: a minimal system of roads in a landscape with a lake.

of coincidence" (the set of points where the object touches the soap film) looks like.

Problems of this kind, called *obstacle problems,* have been an important and fruitful field of mathematical research, and have led to the development of many new and interesting techniques in the calculus of variations. It is obviously useful to study such problems. If, for instance, you plan to connect several cities by a road system of shortest total length, but the roads must avoid some lakes, mountain areas, and national parks, you are faced with a generalization of Steiner's problem that must take obstacles into account (see the figure at the left). The solution of optimality questions under such subsidiary conditions turns out to be one of the most important problems in applied mathematics. We met another type of obstacle problem when we considered minimal surfaces with a free boundary.

Many problems related to the Frei Otto or "thread" experiments have been solved experimentally but not mathematically. For example, what is the highest point that a soap film can reach if it is lifted from a

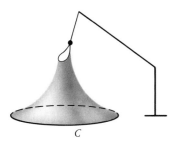

How high can an eye loop lift soap film?

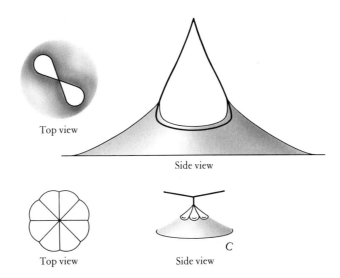

Top view

Side view

Top view   Side view

Minimal surfaces with several eye loops attached to one point.

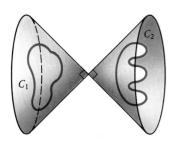

Two cones give a nonexistence result.

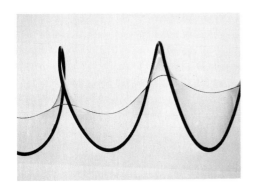

Helix with thread.

planar contour by an eye loop (see the top figure on the left)? We have seen that two curves C_1 and C_2 cannot be spanned by a connected soap film if they are too far apart. In fact, C_1 and C_2 cannot bound such a minimal surface if the two curves can be separated (as in the middle figure on the left) by a circular cone that is generated by revolving a pair of straight lines, meeting at right angles, about an axis of symmetry. Given the length of the eye loop and the position of the exterior contour C, we can thus easily derive an upper bound for the height above the ground of the minimal surface in the top figure on the left; yet it would be interesting to find the exact figure.

We could also attach several loops to the same point (see the figure above), or fix a thread at the end points of a given arc. A soap film will then span the thread in such a way that it minimizes area, and the thread will form a curve of constant curvature where it is not attached to C. The photograph on the left shows a soap film that is bounded in part by a wire in the form of a helix, and in part by a thread tied to some points of the helix.

6

Optimal Design

*Nature does nothing in vain, and more is
in vain when less will serve; for Nature
is pleased with simplicity, and affects not
the pomp of superfluous causes.*

(Isaac Newton, *Principia*)

In the fifth century A.D., the Greek
philosopher Proclus wrote, *"The circle is the first, the most simple, and
the most perfect figure."* The perfect symmetry of the circle justifies
this statement, as does the beautiful isoperimetric property of the circle. As Queen Dido had found, of all plane figures of equal perimeter,
the circle has the maximum area.

We have, however, not yet seen a proof of this theorem; so let us
look at the reasoning given by Jakob Steiner in 1836.

The Isoperimetric Problem

Let us assume that a solution of the isoperimetric problem
exists. Then, we have a *curve C that, among all closed lines of a given
length, encloses the maximal area.* We would like to show that this
curve is a circle. First, we note that it is a convex curve; that is, every
straight connection of two points inside curve C is entirely within the
curve (compare parts A and B of the illustration on the next page).
Otherwise curve C would lie on one side of a straight line, L, that
passes through points P'' and Q'' on the curve, so that those points of L

A calcite twinned crystal from the Elmwood
Mine in Tennessee.

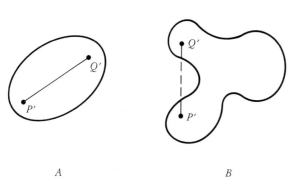

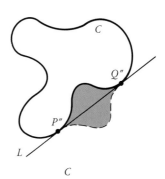

A

B

C

D

A. A convex curve.

B. A nonconvex curve.

C. If C is not convex, then by reflection along L we generate a new curve C*, as shown in part D. This new curve, although the same length as curve C, encloses more area than does C.

that are between P″ and Q″ do not belong to curve C (see part C of the illustration). Then, as indicated in part D, we could construct a new curve C*, which would enclose more area than would curve C but would have the same perimeter. This, however, contradicts our assumption that C encloses maximal area. Hence our solution curve must be convex.

Next, we choose two points R and S on convex curve C such that these points divide C into two arcs of equal length, C′ and C″. The straight line through R and S cuts the interior of C into two pieces, B′ and B″, as shown at the left below. The optimum property of curve C implies that B′ and B″ have the same area. This can be seen as follows. Suppose, for example, that B′ had a larger area than did B″. Then, if we reflected region B′ about line segment RS, we would obtain a new region, the mirror image of B′, as shown below. The union of B′ with its mirror image would then form a figure that had a larger area than that of the interior of C, whereas its perimeter would equal the length of C. This, however, would contradict our assumption about the optimality of curve C; so the areas of B′ and B″ must be equal.

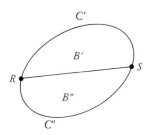

A convex curve divided by two points, R and S, into two arcs, C′ and C″, of equal length.

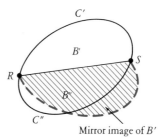

Symmetrization of a convex curve.

Using a mechanical argument to complete the proof of the isoperimetric property of the circle.

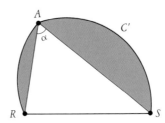 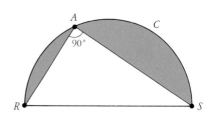

To prove that C is a circle, it suffices to show that both C' and C'' are semicircles. Once more, we will argue by contradiction.

Suppose that one of the two arcs—say, C'—were not a semicircle. Then a classical theorem attributed to Thales would imply that there is a point A on arc C' such that angle α of triangle RAS at corner A is *not* 90°. Imagine now that sides AR and AS could be moved by a hinge installed at A, so that we could reduce or increase the angle at the joint, and, furthermore, that the two lunules (crescent-moon forms) shown in color in the illustration above were rigidly attached to the arms of the hinge, so that they moved with them when they opened or closed. We could then change the opening of the hinge from the original angle, α, to an angle of 90°, thereby increasing the area of triangle RAS. Together with the attached lunules, the new figure would have a larger area than did the old one with angle α at A. Yet the area of the old figure was, as we have seen, half of that of the interior of curve C. Therefore, if we reflected the new figure at the straight line through R and S and unified it with its mirror image, we would obtain a domain with the same circumference as C but with a larger area. This cannot be; so arc C' has to be a semicircle. It follows in the same way that C'' is a semicircle, and therefore C is a circle.

We thus have proved that the circle is the only solution to the isoperimetric problem. For Steiner, the problem was solved at this stage. Reportedly, his colleague Dirichlet tried without success to convince him that the proof was not complete. As we have seen, the existence of a solution of a reasonable geometric problem is by no means obvious; in fact, sometimes a solution may not even exist. For the isoperimetric problem, however, the existence of a solution can be verified. Thus, *the only curve that maximizes area among all closed lines of the same perimeter is the circle.* We will not present the existence proof because it is beyond the scope of this book.

We can draw a very interesting conclusion from the isoperimetric property of the circle. To this end, consider an arbitrary closed curve C of perimeter L. Suppose that it encloses a domain of area A. Let r be the radius of a circle of perimeter L; that is, $L = 2\pi r$. Such a circle encloses a disc with an area of πr^2. By the isoperimetric property of the circle, the area A of the curve C cannot be larger than πr^2, and it equals πr^2 if and only if C is a circle. On the other hand, we have

$$\pi r^2 = \frac{1}{4\pi}(2\pi r)^2 = \frac{1}{4\pi}L^2,$$

and we thus obtain the celebrated *isoperimetric inequality*

$$A \le \frac{1}{4\pi}L^2$$

between the perimeter L of an arbitrary closed plane curve and the area A of its interior, where the equality sign holds only for the circle.

The isoperimetric inequality has the following theorem as a consequence:

Among all plane figures of equal area, the disc has minimal perimeter.

This can easily be seen, because the area A of a disc of perimeter L^* equals $L^{*2}/4\pi$. If there were a plane figure with the same area but with a smaller perimeter L than that of the disc, we would have $A > L^2/4\pi$, which contradicts the isoperimetric inequality.

This statement gives another equivalent formulation of the isoperimetric property of the circle. It also explains why the oil drops on your broth are circular, not triangular or hexagonal. The molecular forces generate a figure of least circumference—that is, of smallest potential energy for a given amount of oil—and this is a disc. If two floating oil drops hit each other, they quickly merge into a single larger oil drop.

Not surprisingly, there are several other optimum properties of the circle. For instance, *among all plane domains of a given area, the disc can support the largest sand pile*. This may prove to be valuable information for your children or grandchildren if they are at the age to build castles of sand.

A very similar problem arises in the theory of plasticity: *What should the cross section of a perfectly elastic column be in order to withstand the largest torsional moment (that is, the largest amount of twisting)?* Again, the cross section must be circular.

Another beautiful feature of the disc was observed by the British physicist Lord Rayleigh. It concerns the musical sound generated by a membrane, for example, by beating a drum. As you may know, you can lower the principal frequency of the membrane by "increasing its size," say, by increasing its area. It would then be interesting to learn which membrane, out of all plane membranes with a given area, has the lowest principal frequency; that is, *which drum, out of all drums with a given cross-sectional area, has the lowest tone?* By experiment, Rayleigh (1877) was led to conjecture that a circular membrane has this minimum property, but it took almost half a century until this conjecture was proved by Faber and Krahn (1923/24).

Similarly, *among all clamped plates of given area, the disc-shaped one has the minimal principal frequency.*

In fact, the field of acoustics provides many other interesting applications for the calculus of variations. We can even say that the theory of pure tones, the very field of Pythagorean physics, is nothing but a subdomain of variational calculus.

Balls and Bubbles

For mathematicians, a ball is a solid with a sphere as its surface. It is a perfectly round body that looks the same from all sides. For a homogeneous ball, the geometric center coincides with the center of gravity. Therefore, on a horizontal plane, the equilibrium position of such a ball is always undecided. It can rest in all positions; yet the slightest kick, in any direction whatsoever, will cause it to roll. Furthermore, we are never sure what path it will take, since a tiny unevenness of the ground could make it turn. Thus the ball became one of the attributes of the capricious goddess Fortuna.

Another symbol of fortune is the soap bubble. This airy creation is, as long as it lasts, a consequence of Bernoulli's law of virtual work. This law, as we have seen, requires that in stable equilibrium the potential energy has to be a minimum. In a soap bubble, some amount of air is enclosed by a surface of minimum area, the soap film. This is the physical evidence for the mathematical theorem that, *out of all solids of a given volume, the ball has the smallest surface area,* a result that is the obvious spatial analogue of a minimum property of the circle: Among all plane figures of a given area, the circle has the shortest perimeter.

Albrecht Dürer's "Small Fortune."

Ion exchanger: a synthetic or natural material that can exchange ions between itself and its environment. For example, water can be softened by removing calcium, magnesium, and carbonate ions from it.

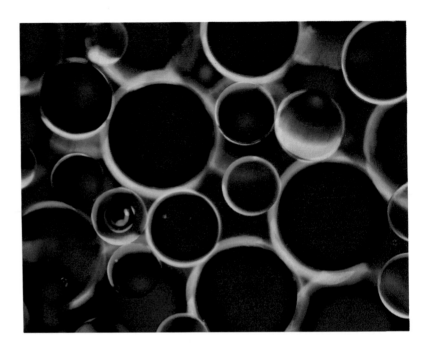

For the same reason, globules of oil suspended in a liquid of the same density (or brought into outer space, which is nearly free of gravitational forces) will form perfect balls. This can be seen in experiments, and the corresponding mathematical theorem has been rigorously proved.

In 1919, the Swedish mathematician Torsten Carleman showed that the ball is the only equilibrium figure for a self-gravitating liquid at rest. In huge masses, the powerful forces of self-attraction predicted by Newton's law dominate other forces, such as surface tension, which can then be disregarded. Let us suppose that the planets arose from liquid masses that hardened as they cooled. The ball is then the only shape that a planet at rest could have achieved. The situation is different if the celestial body is rotating, as do the Earth, the other planets, and their satellites. We shall consider this situation later on.

Recall that a ball of radius r has a volume $V = \frac{1}{3}\pi r^3$ and a surface area $A = 4\pi r^2$, from which we obtain the relation $36\pi V^2 = A^3$. We can then employ an argument similar to the proof of the isoperimetric inequality to derive the inequality

$$V^2 \leq \frac{1}{36\pi}A^3$$

between the volume V of an arbitrary solid and its surface area A, where equality holds only for balls. This estimate is the spatial version of the isoperimetric inequality. Therefore, we have the following maximum property of the ball: *Of all solids with prescribed surface area, the ball has the largest volume.*

We can change the problem of finding surfaces of least area enclosing a prescribed volume by adding suitable boundary conditions. For example, we may consider the problem of finding the solid of largest volume with a prescribed surface area when the part of the boundary contained in some given plane is not counted. The solution is a half-ball, as we can prove by a reflection argument.

The following problem is closely related. Consider a solid wedged between parallel planes. The *reduced surface area* of such a body consists of those parts of the surface that do not lie on either plane. *For a given value of reduced surface area, what is the solid of maximum volume wedged between two planes?* Equivalently, *what wedged solid of a fixed volume has the least possible reduced surface area?*

We can solve this problem experimentally by blowing a soap bubble between two wetted glass plates. Let us begin with a bubble in the form of a hemisphere that sits on one of the wetted plates. As we blow more air into the hemisphere, we enlarge it until it also touches the second plate, whereupon it changes into a circular cylinder that sits perpendicularly on both plates and meets them in circles, as shown in the illustration at the left. Then, by the same reasoning as that used for the "experimental" solution of Steiner's problem, we can conclude that the circle is the shortest curve that encloses a given area. As we have seen, this fact is equivalent to the isoperimetric property of the circle.

We can use the plate experiment to establish an interesting connection between the Steiner problem and the isoperimetric problem. Suppose that we have two glass plates connected by three parallel pins of equal length that meet both planes perpendicularly. Then, using a straw, we blow a cylindrical soap bubble between the two wetted planes such that the cylindrical soap film contains all three pins as shown in the illustraton at the left below.

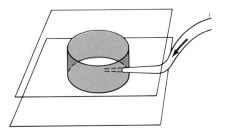

Soap-film demonstration of the isoperimetric property of the circle.

A cylindrical soap bubble between two plates held apart by three pins of equal length demonstrates the relation between Steiner's problem and the isoperimetric property of the circle.

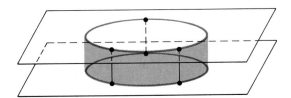

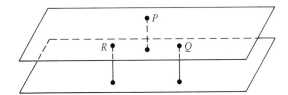

Changes in configuration of the cylindrical
soap bubble as air is being withdrawn
from it.

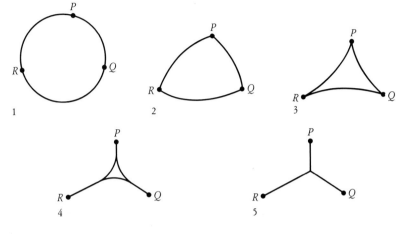

Then we slowly draw air out of the bubble. The cylindrical shape
will continuously change through a sequence of configurations, and
eventually will become a system of three soap films that meet both
glass plates perpendicularly. The liquid edges of the soap-film configurations at various stages during this procedure are illustrated above;
this, as we see, connects the isoperimetric with the Steiner problem.
Note that in each configuration the liquid edges are either straight or
circular arcs, because only plane and cylindrical soap films will arise.

A nearly cubical bubble within a bubble cluster, created by Tom Noddy.

A near dodecahedron within a bubble cluster, created by Tom Noddy.

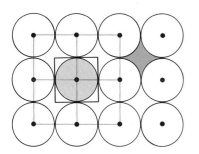

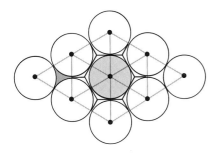

Tightest packing of circles. The hexagonal packing of discs (say, coins) minimizes the space left between them relative to the space left in a square array (as in the lower drawing).

Now let us put circular cylinders of the same size on a plate and try to arrange them in a closed packing. Then we will obtain a hexagonal pattern, because this provides the tightest packing of circular objects of the same size in the plane (see the upper illustration in the margin, in which the central circle touches exactly six neighbors). This interesting property is another reason why the hexagon, the 120° angle, and the Y-shape so often occur in nature.

Similarly, balls of equal size between two plates, densely packed, arrange themselves in a hexagonal array. Imagine each ball to be a living cell that tries to expand as much as possible, and each by the same amount. Then it seems obvious that a pattern of hexagonal cells will form. In fact, this is what we very often see with cell growth, and exterior pressure may lead to the same result if it is uniformly applied.

Packing of soap bubbles.

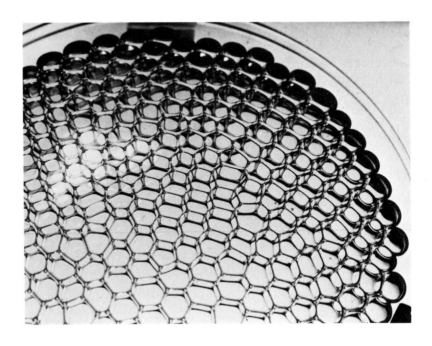

However, the hexagonal pattern can also be obtained in a completely different way. Let us blow soap bubbles of the same size between two parallel plates. The bubbles will soon unite. According to rules 1 and 2 for systems of soap films, which apply to this situation as well, we then obtain a system of soap films with liquid edges that obey the 90° and the 120° law. Moreover, if the bubbles are of the same size, there is no pressure difference between two adjacent cells; so all interior films must have mean curvature zero—in fact, they are planar surfaces. Hence we get an array of hexagonal cells where only the outermost films are cylindrical, because for them there is a pressure difference between the outside and the inside of the cell (see the photograph above).

We see that the hexagonal pattern may form for different reasons; that is, the configuration of minimal area can be generated by very different forces, such as uniform pressure or surface tension. *Therefore it is impossible to deduce from the pattern what forces are acting on it.*

Nevertheless, as the naturalist D'Arcy Thompson pointed out in *On Growth and Form*, exactly such careless deductions have been made by scientists when they wanted to explain the geometric structure of the beehive. As we all know, one of the most beautiful hexagonal arrays is the honeycomb constructed by bees. The writings of Pappus inform us that the ancient Greeks had already tried to explain the regularity of beehive cells by means of an optimum principle. The French physicist R. A. F. de Réaumur (1683–1757) also thought that the hexagonal structure of the bee's honeycomb should follow from a minimum principle: the bee would build its cells with the greatest economy in order to use as little wax as possible. Réaumur posed his conjecture to Samuel Koenig, the later adversary of Maupertuis. Koenig found that the angles of 120° and of 109°26′ followed from the minimum principle proposed by Réaumur, and these seemed to agree with the actual measurements of the bee cells. Thereupon Fontenelle, the secretary of the French Academy, declared that bees had no intelligence; yet they were *"blindly using the highest mathematics by divine guidance and command."* On this D'Arcy Thompson commented that it makes more sense to suppose *"that the beautiful regularity of the bee's architecture is due to some automatic play of the physical forces"* than to suppose *"that the bee intentionally seeks for a method of economizing wax."*

But all this assumes that the bees *have* somehow hit upon the optimal honeycomb. Have they? This question was investigated by the Hungarian mathematician Fejes Tóth in 1964. In his paper "What the bees know and what they don't know," he considered *honeycombs,* which he defined as a set of congruent convex polyhedra, called *cells,* filling the space between two parallel planes without overlapping and without interstices in such a way that: (1) each cell has a face (called a *base* or *opening*) on one and only one of the two planes; and (2) every pair of cells is congruent in such a way that their bases correspond to each other.

The cells built by the bees are prismatic vessels, the openings (and cross sections) of which are regular hexagons, whereas their bottoms consist of three equal rhombi (see part *D* of the illustration on the next page). The bees construct their honeycomb in such a way that the hexagonal openings of the cells are attached to one of the two planes. Is the zigzagged bottom surface constructed by the bees the most economical one? (It is certainly more advantageous than a plane.)

In order to state the problem precisely, we formulate (following Fejes Tóth) the *isoperimetric problem for honeycombs:*

Given any two numbers V and W, find a honeycomb of width W whose cells have smallest surface area and yet enclose the volume V.

(The width W is the distance between the two parallel planes that bound the honeycomb.)

A. Honeycomb.
B. Longitudinal section.
C. Cross section.
D. An individual cell.

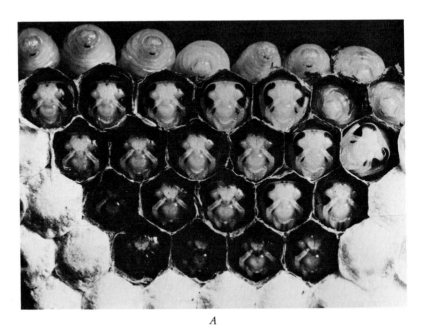

A

B

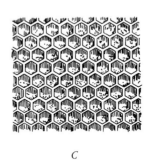

C

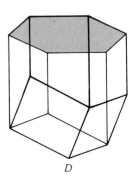

D

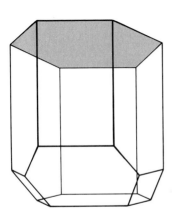

Fejes Tóth's cell.

We don't know yet what the solution will be, but definitely it cannot be the bee cell, because Fejes Tóth found another cell that yields a slightly better result. The bottom of this cell consists of two hexagons and two rhombi (see the illustration at the left). The savings of Tóth's cell is less than 0.35% of the area of an opening (and a much smaller percentage of the surface area of a cell). Hence we can state that the bees do a pretty good but not perfect job, although their practical result, taking the margin of error into account, might still be optimal.

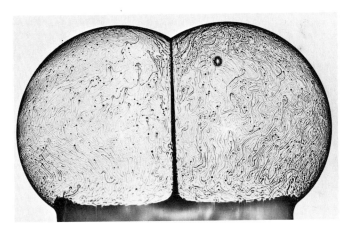

Two bubbles on a plate.

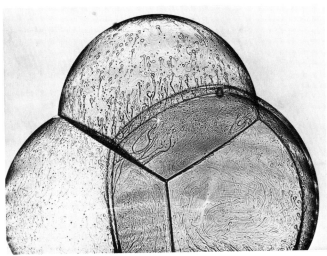

Four bubbles.

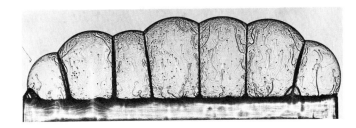

A "worm" of seven bubbles.

Let us return to a consideration of the many configurations of soap films, soap bubbles, or combinations of soap films and soap bubbles that span frames of various kinds. We can use wires, glass plates, or surfaces of liquids on which the bubble configurations will rest or float. We can also combine supporting surfaces, curves (wires), and movable lines (threads). Some possible configurations are shown above and on the next two pages.

Consider the mathematical problem of describing soap bubbles or configurations of soap films and soap bubbles. As we already know, the problem is to minimize surface area among all configurations con-

A "worm" of seventeen bubbles produced by Tom Noddy, whose record stands at eighteen bubbles.

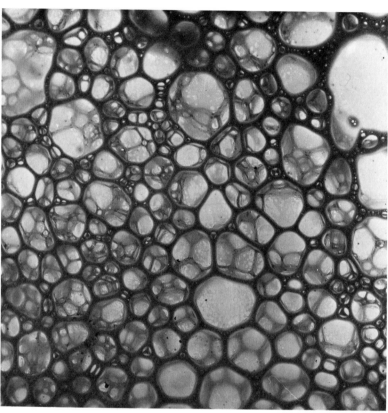

A conglomeration of bubbles, or foam.

sisting of surfaces that span a given framework (rigid or movable) and enclose some prescribed volume. The solutions of such a mathematical problem consist of one or more surfaces of constant mean curvature, *H*. Minimal surfaces are those whose mean curvature is zero, whereas spheres and cylinders have constant mean curvatures different from zero. *Thus the solutions of the mathematical model problems are conglomerates of surfaces with different mean curvatures.* They are models of the soap-film/soap-bubble arrays observed in experiments. Minimal surfaces correspond to soap films exposed to the same pressure on both sides, whereas surfaces whose mean curvature is not zero correspond to soap films exposed to more pressure on one side than on the other.

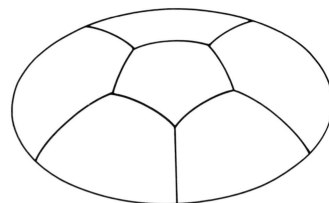

Bubbles in threads (above) and diagram of threads (above right).

Although such surfaces are a good approximation to physical reality, they should not be identified with it. It is essential that we distinguish the physical phenomenon from its mathematical model, particularly because the mathematical concept may encompass a much larger realm of objects than we can actually realize by experiment. If, for example, a surface of constant mean curvature lacks stability, it cannot be physically embodied in a soap film. We have already seen that there are unstable minimal surfaces (for example, certain catenoids) that cannot be physically embodied in soap films. Similarly, the cylinder surface becomes unstable if its length equals or exceeds its circumference, which is π times its diameter. This can be easily demonstrated by an experiment that, however, requires some delicacy (see the legend on the next page). Consider a cylindrical soap film between two coaxial rings. As soon as the cylindrical film becomes unstable, it will decompose into two separate, spherical soap bubbles of different sizes. The instability of long cylinders can be not only demonstrated by experiment, but also proved rigorously in the mathematical model.

The cylindrical soap bubble's instability, which was discovered by Plateau, is closely related to a similar physical phenomenon that everyone knows: every jet of water breaks into a series of water droplets. We can observe this phenomenon at a fountain or by watching a sprinkler in a garden. The dispersion of water jets into a spray of droplets is very sensitive to perturbations like those caused by electrical fields or sound vibrations. In his classic *Soap Bubbles, Their Colours, and the Forces Which Mold Them*, the British physicist C.V. Boys describes many simple experiments that can be done with water jets or soap bubbles. Boys's book grew out of three lectures given in

Soap bubbles between two coaxial rings. They usually are not cylinders but have developed a waist or, as in the pictures above, a bulge. (An explanation of this phenomenon is found on pages 161–163.) To obtain cylinders from the bubbles with a waist or a bulge, we must either add or extract air.

1889/90 by this outstanding experimentalist, who occasionally enjoyed shooting enormous smoke rings at startled pedestrians from the windows of his laboratory in an effort to surround them by the rings.

Let us now illustrate the difference between reality and mathematical model again by considering a seemingly simple example, the spherical soap bubble. Nature has no difficulty showing that spheres are the only smooth soap bubbles (without an artificial boundary) that you can blow into the air. However, until 1984, we did not know whether *spheres are the only complete finite surfaces of constant mean curvature.* (The unlimited cylinder, also a complete surface of constant mean curvature, is not finite; it extends to infinity in both directions.) Most mathematicians conjectured that the answer was, "Yes, spheres are the only ones," and various partial results were proved. We knew, for example, that spheres were the only *convex* surfaces of constant mean curvature among the finite complete surfaces. A. D. Alexandrov even proved that a non-self-intersecting handle-body surface of finite genus cannot have constant mean curvature. Yet mathematicians wanted to obtain a completely general result. For this purpose, surfaces with self-intersections also must be taken into consideration. Admitting such surfaces, Heinz Hopf was able to show that finite surfaces of genus zero and without boundary must be spheres, even if they have self-intersections. Very recently, however, the conjecture has been disproved: there exists a complete finite surface of genus one and of constant mean curvature but with self-intersections.

Closed curve (A) without self-intersection and
(B) with it.
Closed surface (C) without self-intersection
and (D) with it.

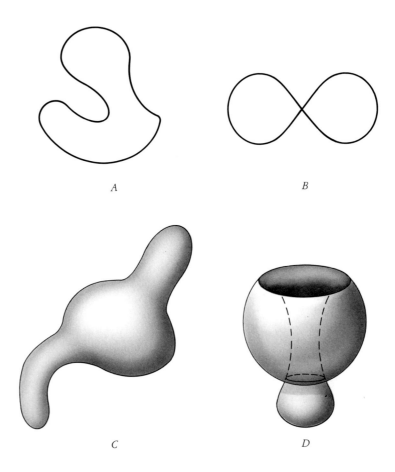

A

B

C

D

Rotationally Symmetric Surfaces
of Constant Mean Curvature

Because surfaces of constant mean curvature are the models
of soap films and soap bubbles, it would be interesting to know which
of them are also rotationally symmetric, as are the disc, the catenoid,
and the cylinder. We shall call them *H-surfaces of revolution*. Plateau
had found that there are exactly six different kinds of *H*-surfaces of
revolution: the plane and the catenoid (mean curvature zero), the
sphere, the cylinder, the unduloid, and the nodoid (mean curvature
nonzero). In 1841, the French mathematician Delaunay proved that

Plateau's list of *H*-surfaces of revolution was indeed complete and that, moreover, all of them could be generated by a simple rule, which can be described as follows. We fix some straight line to serve as the *axis of rotation*. Thereafter, we choose a conic section—that is, an ellipse, a circle, a parabola, or a hyperbola—and we imagine that the conic section rolls on the axis. Each focus of the conic section will then describe a curve called the *roulade* of the focus. When rotated about the axis, this curve generates in space one of the six *H*-surfaces of revolution. Five of the generating curves are shown at the left.

For example, the focus of a circle describes a straight line parallel to the axis, and the corresponding surface of revolution is a *cylinder*.

If an ellipse rolls on the axis, either of its foci generates an undulatory (wavy) curve that never touches the axis, and this curve, when rotated, generates the *unduloid*. If the foci of the ellipse are not very far apart, each of the undulatory curves is only slightly wavy and, if the foci move together, the unduloid more and more closely approximates a cylinder.

The opposite extreme of an ellipse is a straight-line segment, which can be thought of as a degenerate ellipse in which the two foci are as far apart as possible: the two end points of the segment are its foci. The roulade of this line segment is a sequence of semicircles (one end touches down, the other swings around, tracing a semicircle, and so on), which upon rotation generates a sequence of equal *spheres*.

If one focus of the ellipse remains finite but the other moves out to infinity, the ellipse changes into a parabola. The roulade of its focus is a catenary, which is, as we have seen, the meridian of the *catenoid*.

Finally, we will describe how the roulade of one of the foci of a hyperbola is generated. Imagine that the two branches of the hyperbola are rigidly connected, so that they can move only as a unit. Roll one branch of the hyperbola on the upper side of the axis, say, to the right, from one asymptote to the other, * and then the other branch on the lower side of the axis to the right, from one asymptote to the other. By repeating the rolling again and again, moving always to the right, and by following the trace of one of the foci, we obtain a curve that extends infinitely to the right. In a similar way, this curve can be extended infinitely to the left. Thus we obtain a smooth curve with infinitely many loops, which generates the *nodoid* as the surface of revolution.

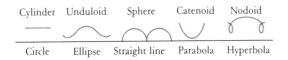

Cylinder Unduloid Sphere Catenoid Nodoid

Circle   Ellipse Straight line Parabola Hyperbola

The generating curves of the *H*-surfaces of revolution. The roulade of a circle generates a cylinder; that of an ellipse generates an unduloid; and so forth.

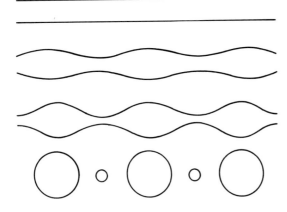

Several *H*-surfaces of revolution (cylinder, unduloids, sphere).

---

*Asymptotes are limiting lines that the branches of the hyperbola approach but never touch.

The *plane* is obtained by rotating a straight line around an axis that intersects it at a right angle. Yet, by a limit consideration, such a perpendicular is seen to be the limit of a sequence of semicircles whose radius is increasing toward infinity. Thus the perpendicular can be interpreted as the roulade of an infinitely long and infinitely thin ellipse.

How to Take a Bath in a Spaceship

As we have seen, the principle of virtual work implies that soap-film configurations consist of surfaces of constant mean curvature. It also follows from this principle that free surfaces of liquids not under the influence of gravitation are such surfaces.

How can we switch off gravitation? Either we can shoot a container with liquid into outer space or we can place it in an elevator, which is then dropped in free fall. The latter experiment has been done and has led to an impressive confirmation of various mathematical predictions.

As you probably realize, astronauts, when in outer space, can encounter strange difficulties caused by the absence of gravity. For example, what would you recommend as a bathtub if the astronauts want to take a bath when there is no gravity?

Clearly the astronauts should not splash water about; they would have a hard time collecting the floating drops and returning them to their container. Yet a more serious difficulty is that bathtubs may not be able to hold wetting liquids in equilibrium ("wetting" refers to pulling forces at the wall of the container). This is what happens: the free surface of a wetting liquid makes a definite *contact angle* γ (which is somewhere between 0° and 90°) with the walls of its container (see the illustrations on the next page). Suppose that the container has a horizontal bottom and vertical side walls, so that all horizontal cross sections look alike. Assume that the side walls have edges, with the interior angle at an edge being α. Then the wetting fluid cannot be in equilibrium within the container if $\alpha/2 + \gamma < 90°$. In other words, an astronaut has a good chance that the water in his bathtub will climb over the upper edges of the container; it will do so if the wetting angle γ is less than 45° and the bathtub has a rectangular cross section.

In many situations, we can assume that the wetting angle γ will be close to zero, say, for glass and a watery liquid. Hence, on your next flight to the Moon, you will spoil your clothes if you try to have your apéritif in a glass with a square cross section. This, by the way, is

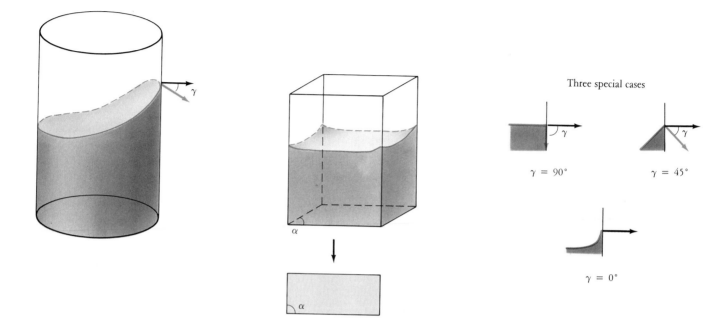

Three special cases

$\gamma = 90°$ $\gamma = 45°$

$\gamma = 0°$

The contact angle γ: three special cases.

not a mathematical fairy tale, because the formula $\alpha/2 + \gamma < 90°$, inferred from theoretical considerations, was well confirmed by experiments carried out at the NASA drop tower.

The illustration at the upper right on the facing page shows the vertical section of the *Astronaut's Bathtub* suggested by Paul Concus and Robert Finn in 1974. The curvy part of the boundary of this section consists of two pieces of the roulade generated by the focus of a hyperbola. The free surface formed by the liquid in the bathtub is displayed in the upper right-hand drawing on the facing page, assuming that the water meets the boundary walls at an angle of 0°; the water level is part of a nodoid.

There is, however, a third way to get rid of gravity: by placing the fluid to be investigated (say, oil) into another liquid (alcohol and water in the right mixture) that will not mix with the first one but has the same density. We can, for example, introduce a small amount of oil by means of a tube or a pipette into the alcohol-water mixture. The oil will immediately form a perfect ball.

Every falling raindrop should, of course, be sphere-shaped, as it would be if the drop were falling in a vacuum. The air resistance, however, causes the falling drop to be nonspherical. Moreover, there is an internal motion in each falling drop.

A liquid has climbed up the walls of its container (experiment devised by Concus and Finn and carried out by Massica at the NASA drop tower, Cleveland, Ohio); $\alpha = 60°$, $\gamma = 25°$.

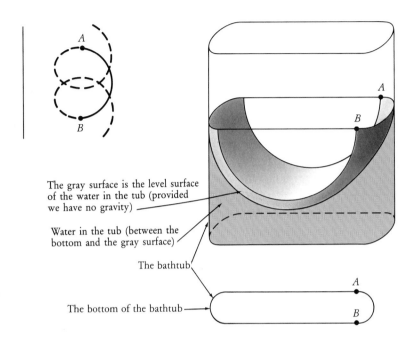

The gray surface is the level surface of the water in the tub (provided we have no gravity)

Water in the tub (between the bottom and the gray surface)

The bathtub

The bottom of the bathtub

Astronaut's bath tub: roulade of hyperbola (left) is the curve to which water will cling (right).

Falling rain drop.

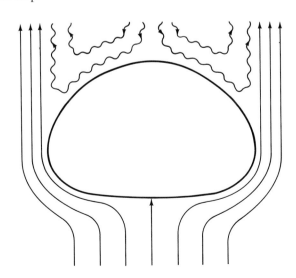

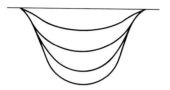

Pendant water drops.

Gravity strongly influences drops. For example, on a glass plate, drops of a nonwetting liquid, like mercury, are nearly spherical if they are very small, whereas larger blobs are fairly flattened by their own weight, and large amounts of mercury flow apart and form a very flat puddle.

The *hanging drops* of a wetting liquid (see the adjacent drawing) are in some ways quite different from *sitting drops*. We all know that a pendant drop cannot be "too large." That is, the elastic skin can hold the weight of only small amounts of liquid, whereas a heavier weight will tear the skin. There is, in fact, a well-defined size to which a pendant drop can grow. When this size is reached, a tiny perturbation will cause the drop to fall. We can also explain this phenomenon by saying the drop has reached its stability limit, and has shifted from a stable to an unstable equilibrium. This is why all drops from a medicine dropper are of the same size. It is worth noting that, about a hundred years ago, numerical investigations of the hanging drop led to the development of powerful numerical techniques that are now widely used by numerical analysts in many fields of applied science.

Planets, Rotating Drops, and the Nuclei of Atoms

Three other phenomena can be explained by a single variational principle founded on Bernoulli's principle of virtual work. These phenomena belong to the fields of astronomy, hydrodynamics, and nuclear physics, which, at first sight, do not seem to have very much in common. Specifically, we will consider *rotating and self-gravitating liquid masses* of homogeneous density; then, *rotating liquid drops endowed with surface tension;* and, finally, the *nuclei of atoms* with or without an angular momentum.

All of these considerations can be subsumed in the following general problem. Imagine some amount of homogeneous fluid, in one or several blobs (or, as mathematicians say, distributed over a connected or a nonconnected domain). Each part of the fluid may be either simply connected (like a ball) or multiply connected (like a handle body, say, a solid ring).

We shall assume that no exterior forces (such as gravity) are exerted on the liquid, but that all active forces are generated by the fluid itself. This does not exclude the phenomenon of *self-gravitation*, which plays a role only for extremely large masses of a liquid. Self-gravitation is caused by the attraction that every part of the liquid has for every other part according to Newton's law of gravitation. This force tends to keep the liquid together. Let us also assume that *surface tension* may play a role. In other words, we consider liquids whose surface is covered by an elastic skin that also exerts a contractive influence on the liquid. Moreover, we will assume that two dispersing forces, electrostatic and centrifugal, work against these forces of attraction. If the liquid carries a *uniform electric charge*, then by Coulomb's law each part will repel every other part. Finally, if the liquid is *rotating with uniform angular velocity* about its center of mass like a gyroscope, each part will be subject to centrifugal forces that tend to disperse the liquid.

A liquid body is said to be in *gyrostatic* (or *relative*) *equilibrium* if it rotates like a gyroscope. An observer sitting somewhere within the liquid and having no connection to the exterior world would not notice the rotation; he would think that the body were at rest.

Thus, in gyrostatic equilibrium, four kinds of forces are balancing each other: the contractive forces of *surface tension* and *self-gravitation* counterbalance the dispersive *electrostatic* and *centrifugal* forces.

The obvious questions to ask are, *What are the possible shapes of liquid bodies in gyrostatic equilibrium?* Moreover, *which bodies are in stable gyrostatic equilibrium?*

According to Bernoulli's *principle of virtual work*, the equilibria are the stationary states of the potential energy, and the stable equilibria correspond to the minima of potential energy.

The total potential energy of a liquid body is the sum of four terms:

$$Total\ energy\ =\ surface\ energy\ +\ gravitational\ energy\\ +\ electrostatic\ energy\ +\ rotational\ energy$$

in which the potential energy of surface tension is in proportion to the surface area of the liquid body and the term "rotational energy" denotes the potential energy of the centrifugal forces.

Historically, the earliest example considered was that of rotating bodies of liquids, which served as models of the planets and, later on, of the stars and nebulae. Here the forces of self-attraction caused by gravitation are so enormously large that the influence of surface tension can be neglected. At first only uncharged celestial bodies were considered and for these the potential energy reduces to the sum of gravitational and rotational energy.

The theory of rotating celestial bodies started with the work of Isaac Newton, Colin MacLaurin, and Alexis-Claude Clairaut. However, experimental observations of the rotation of celestial bodies had, in fact, been made much earlier.

The dark spots of the Sun had long been observed without the use of telescopes, and it was known that they actually changed their positions. In the European latitudes, the sunspots move from the left-hand side to the right-hand side of the Sun. These observations became much more accurate when astronomers were able to view the Sun with a refracting telescope. In 1611 the German astronomer Fabricius concluded from his observations that the spots were integral parts of the Sun and that their movement was caused by the *Sun's rotation*—a dramatic discovery! In 1612 Galileo in Italy, Thomas Harriot in England, and the German Jesuit Christoph Scheiner published their own observations. Galileo came forth with the same explanation of the movement of the spots as did Fabricius, whereas Scheiner said they were small planets revolving around the Sun. In his 1613 publication *Istoria e dimostrazioni intorno alle macchie solarie e loro accidenti*, Galileo disproved Scheiner's reasoning and, for the first time, publicly supported the heliocentric theory of Copernicus. Scheiner, who eventually conceded that Galileo was right, went on to make much more accurate observations than Galileo had, and he found that the Sun completes a full rotation in 27 days.

The mathematical theory of rotating stars began with Newton's *Principia*, which demonstrates that a slowly rotating liquid body must necessarily be flattened at the poles (the two points that determine the axis of rotation). We have seen how the verification of this prediction by Maupertuis finally led to the acceptance of Newtonian physics. Voltaire, who had at first enthusiastically congratulated Maupertuis for his achievement, later wrote the malicious verse

> You have confirmed at places boring and muddy
> What Newton knew without moving from his study.

What could an equilibrium configuration of a rotating homogeneous liquid body of a given volume V be? The simplest spatial configuration other than the sphere would be the *oblate spheroid*. This is a body generated by an ellipse that is revolved about its minor axis, as shown at the left.

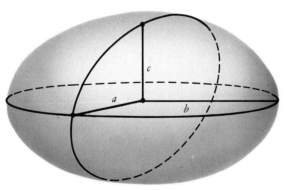

Oblate spheroid, in which the axis of rotation is the minor axis of the ellipse and the major axis is therefore the radius of the circular cross section of the spheroid.

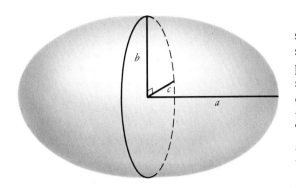

Generic ellipsoid with principal axes and with principal radii a, b, c.

The spheroid is a special case of a (solid) *ellipsoid*, the planar sections of which are all bounded by ellipses (or by circles, which are special cases of the ellipse). Every ellipsoid has *three principal axes*, perpendicular to each other, that pass through the center of the ellipsoid. The *principal radii a, b, c* are the distances from the center to the end points of the principal axes on the surface of the ellipsoid. Let a be the largest and c the smallest of these three numbers—that is, $a \geq b \geq c$. Then a is the largest and c the smallest distance from the center to the surface. An oblate spheroid is characterized by the relation $a = b > c$, whereas a prolate spheroid satisfies $a > b = c$.

In 1742, when essentially no general theory of fluid equilibrium had been developed, Colin MacLaurin showed the following beautiful result:

> For every volume V and for each angular velocity ω which is not too large, there exist two different rotating oblate spheroids that are in gyrostatic equilibrium.

Here "not too large" means that the angular velocity should not exceed

$$\omega_L = 1.188 \sqrt{GD},$$

in which D denotes the density of the liquid and G is Newton's constant of gravitation. If ω tends to the limit ω_L, then the shapes of both MacLaurin spheroids approach that of the same rotating spheroid that rotates with the angular velocity ω_L.

As ω approaches a value of zero (that is, as the rotation slows down to zero), one branch of the MacLaurin spheroids will increasingly resemble a ball of volume V, the well-known equilibrium configuration at absolute rest ($\omega = 0$), whereas the other branch will grow into a disc of "infinite diameter."

For nearly a century it was believed that MacLaurin's spheroids were the only shapes possible for uniformly rotating bodies of homogeneous fluids in gyrostatic equilibrium. Lagrange claimed that there could not be any other equilibrium configurations; yet this was not true. In 1834, Jacobi discovered that,

> For every volume V and every value ω of the angular velocity which is neither zero nor too large, there exists an equilibrium configuration in the shape of an asymmetric ellipsoid ($a > b > c$) that rotates about the axis of the smallest principal radius c.

This means, to be precise, that ω should stay below

$$\omega_J = 1.084 \ \sqrt{GD}.$$

Note that ω_J is less than ω_L.

If ω approaches the value of ω_J, the Jacobi ellipsoid will eventually resemble one of the MacLaurin spheroids (which rotate with the angular velocity ω_J) and, if ω approaches a value of zero, the Jacobi ellipsoid will come to resemble a needle of infinite length. What would life be like on a planet that was very thin and very long, and that rotated very, very slowly?

Another exciting event was a discovery made in 1885 by Henri Poincaré (1854–1912). He found that a new branch of pear-shaped equilibrium configurations bifurcates from the family of Jacobi ellipsoids much as the Jacobi ellipsoids branch off one class of the MacLaurin spheroids. Poincaré conjectured *"that the bifurcation of the pear-shaped body leads onward stably and continuously to a planet attended by a satellite."* He furthermore proclaimed that along the Jacobi sequence there must be other points of bifurcation that give rise to other stable branches that would eventually develop into planets with two, three, or more satellites. In this way Poincaré envisioned a grand scheme that could explain the birth of our solar system by an evolutionary process rather than by sudden catastrophes.

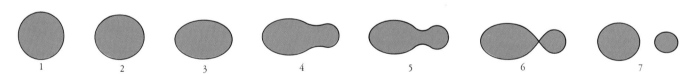

1   2   3   4   5   6   7

The Poincaré bifurcation, with pear-shaped body.

If we follow the cosmogonic hypotheses of Kant and Laplace, our solar system was at first a huge and slowly rotating gas ball of very low density. Self-gravitation would then lead to a contraction of the gas, thereby increasing density and angular velocity, with the matter then changing from a gaseous into a liquid state. As density and speed increased, the originally sphere-shaped matter would become a more and more oblate MacLaurin spheroid, until the bifurcation point of the Jacobi ellipsoids was reached. At this point, the MacLaurin ellipsoids lose their stability, whereas the Jacobi ellipsoids are stable configurations. For this reason, the liquid body would change into a Jacobi ellipsoid and then, with even stronger contraction, into a pear-shaped body, which eventually would fission into a main body and a satellite.

Yet Poincaré never made the detailed calculations necessary to substantiate such a scenario. Such calculations were instead carried out by George Darwin (1845–1912), who claimed that he had proved the stability of the pear forms. Unfortunately, Alexander Lyapunov (1857–1918) was able to refute Darwin's calculations, and other scientists reached the same conclusion. Thus Poincaré's wonderful model collapsed. Nevertheless, the theory of equilibrium configurations developed by Poincaré, Lyapunov, and, later, Lichtenstein was the beginning of *bifurcation theory* in nonlinear analysis. This important theory is a principal tool in such diverse areas as fluid mechanics, mathematical biology, and elasticity theory.

To return to our spinning ball of liquid: it was also known that a figure cannot be in gyrostatic equilibrium if its angular velocity ω is too large. There is, in fact, no possible gyrostatic equilibrium if ω^2 is greater than $2\pi GD$. The only way out of this dilemma is to consider rotating liquid bodies in which the liquid is in internal motion, but whose shape does not alter. This is a much "weaker type" of equilibrium, but very likely a more realistic one. It was studied by Dirichlet and Riemann in the years 1858/60. This work was completed by Chandrasekhar in the 1960s.

Let us now consider small drops of oil that, as devised by Plateau, are suspended in another liquid of the same density. Surface tension is then the dominating force, whereas self-attraction is virtually nil. We moreover assume the oil drop to be uncharged. Here the potential energy is the sum of surface and rotational energy (the influence of the friction of the hosting liquid is neglected).

To follow Plateau's experiments, imagine that a suspended oil drop is touched by a small disc, as shown below. This disc is attached to a thin wire and can thereby be rotated, thus causing the drop to rotate by friction. With increasing angular velocity, the influence of

Plateau's apparatus for rotating drops in a liquid.

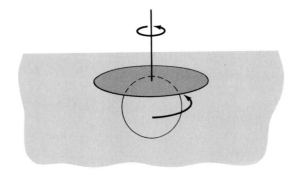

A rotating drop decomposes first into a drop and ring, then into a drop with droplet satellites.

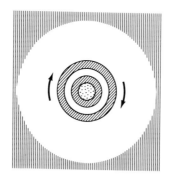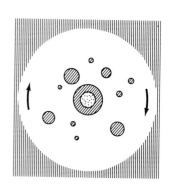

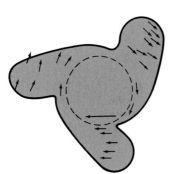

Three-lobed figure; arrows show angular velocity of tracers within drop.

the centrifugal forces will become stronger and stronger. First, the oil drop will flatten at the poles and develop a swelling at the equator. At even higher speed, a ring will separate from the drop (see the illustration above) but will rejoin the central drop when the speed diminishes. However, if the speed increases even more, the ring breaks up into several small drops of *different sizes*.

This circumstance brings to mind a solar system with a large central body circled by smaller satellites. The ring resembles the rings of Saturn or Jupiter. This experiment, however, does not permit us to draw any conclusion about our solar system, because the forces acting in the two situations are rather different.

Recently, Plateau's experiments were repeated and improved on by scientists at the Jet Propulsion Laboratory in Pasadena. Besides the axisymmetric and ring-shaped figures of Plateau, they discovered two-, three- and four-lobed equilibrium shapes. With increasing speed, all figures were seen to decay into a one-lobed shape. No satisfactory method of explaining all this is currently available, because, in fact, the friction between the host liquid and the oil drop cannot be neglected. This friction causes internal flows, which become rather significant as soon as lobes form.

Finally, let us look at the nuclei of atoms. In 1929, George Gamow developed the first model for nuclei, the *drop model*. We can picture a nucleus as a uniformly charged drop with surface tension, either at rest or, in the more subtle model, rotating. The illustration at the top of the facing page depicts the potential-energy landscape for a nonrotating nucleus. Here potential energy is shown as "height" above the corresponding states of the nucleus. The drop will be at the absolute minimum of potential energy if it takes the shape of a ball. If there were no charge, two or any number of balls would also furnish a

Energy landscape.

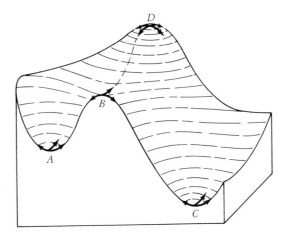

local minimum of the potential energy. However, if the balls are charged, they will repel each other and will be driven to infinity. Thus several balls "at infinity" (that is, sufficiently far away from each other) are also equilibrium configurations, and the "mountain-pass lemma" tells us that there must be a saddle (mountain pass) in the energy landscape somewhere between the "pits" that represent the one or more charged balls at infinity. This mountain pass represents a physical state of unstable equilibrium. In an energy landscape that has a single pit corresponding to a spherical configuration separated by a pass from the binary valley of two balls at infinity, the pass corresponds to a symmetric hourglass figure with two equal bulbs. The shape of the hourglass figure depends on the value of a physical parameter (see below). The height of the saddle point above the single-sphere pit is the *energy barrier* that separates the single-sphere nucleus from

Various hourglass figures corresponding to different values of the physical parameters.

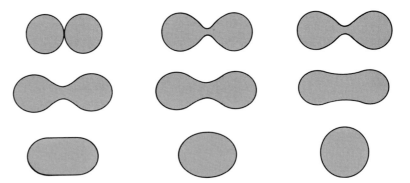

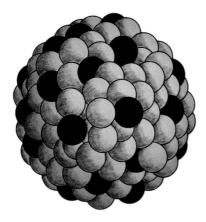

Above: The form of a nucleus at rest in the drop model.
Above right: Various forms of a vibrating nucleus.

fission. If we introduce energy into the nucleus—say, by bumping it with a neutron—we can create vibrations of the nucleus; if these move it above the energy barrier, the nucleus will then be split into two parts.

The Form of Cells

Here let us consider the influence and formative power of physical forces on living beings. This is a vast field, full of unexpected marvels, and we cannot do much more than present some fascinating examples and draw your attention to D'Arcy Thompson's *On Growth and Form*. Although this work was never in the mainstream of biological research and, moreover, disregarded genetics and biochemistry alike, it has become a classic in natural philosophy. Biologists have conceded that it has had a great, though "intangible and indirect," influence. Mathematicians, on the other hand, were and still are fascinated by Thompson's considerations.

The form, then, of any portion of matter, whether it be living or dead, and the changes of form which are apparent in its movements and its growth, may in all cases alike be described as due to the action of force. In short, the form of an object is a "diagram of forces," in this sense, at least, that from it we can judge of or deduce the forces that are acting or have acted upon it: in this strict and particular sense, it is a diagram—in the case of a solid, of the forces which have been impressed upon it when its conformation was produced, together with those which enable it to retain its conformation; in the case of a liquid (or of a gas), of the forces which are for the moment acting on it to restrain or balance its own inherent mobility. In an organism, great or small, it is not merely the nature of the motions of the living substance which we must interpret in terms of force (according to kinetics), but also the conformation of the organism itself, whose permanence or equilibrium is explained by the interaction or balance of forces, as described in statics.

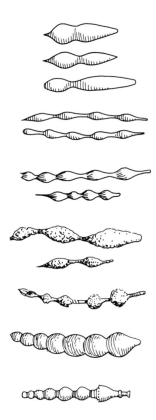

H-surfaces of revolution as unicellulars (compare with the illustration on page 162).

We should bear in mind that biological phenomena are exceedingly complex, and that not everything which seems obvious is true. We should take the mathematical models of these phenomena only as metaphors, and not as "laws" as in astronomy or physics. The day, however, may come when biological forms and processes can be described with the same mathematical precision as those in physics.

Let us consider the influence of surface tension on unicellular beings. They are, crudely speaking, drops of protoplasm, of a very viscous fluid, which are suspended in water. We therefore should expect them to be of spherical shape. This is what we, in fact, see with many simple organisms.

However, as Thompson observed, the spherical forms are usually passive, whereas the unicellular entities that differ greatly from sphericity seem to be rather mobile, and quite often possess little whips in the form of flagella or cilia. In Thompson's opinion, these whips tend to support forms that would otherwise be unstable, and they seem to play a role like that of the boundary configurations (frames) in experiments with soap films and soap bubbles. Moreover, Thompson found all types of *H*-surfaces of revolution among unicellulars. These forms, as he noted, would often have been unstable if it were not for the cilia in permanent motion at the "free edges."

He was cautious enough to state that it is not clear whether *true surface tension* is responsible for all these phenomena or whether *membrane tension* might play a role (unlike a liquid film with surface tension, a membrane contracts just so much, then no more). Modern experimental work has indeed shown that both kinds of tension act in the boundary of a cell. But, as Thompson remarked, within wide limits both forces produce very similar forms.

Thompson also investigated the silicious skeletons of the radiolarians and made a step toward explaining how these skeletons might be formed. He compared the radiolarian body with a

frothy protoplasm, bubbled up into a multitude of alveoli or vacuoles [small cavities], filled with a fluid which can scarcely differ much from sea water, . . . According to their surface-tension conditions, these vacuoles may appear more or less isolated and spherical, or joined together in a "froth" of polyhedral cells; and in the latter, which is the commoner condition, the cells tend to be of equal size, and the resulting polygonal meshwork beautifully regular.

(A bubble froth has to satisfy the two rules, found experimentally by Plateau, that were described earlier.)

Thompson then suggested that adsorption forces were particularly strong in the edges of the froth, which therefore lead to the deposition of inorganic materials along these edges, thus creating the silicious framework of the radiolarian skeleton. Hence *the marvelous regularity of the skeleton was nothing but the materialization of Plateau's two rules.* This suggestion, however, does not explain why there are so many different kinds of skeleton forms among the many species of radiolarians. We are still as puzzled as Ernst Haeckel must have been when he made 4,700 drawings of the radiolarians that he had studied under his microscope. Yet these little "orchids of the sea," as they have been called, are surely no joke of evolution. On the contrary, since radiolarians are among the oldest living beings on earth, they are a kind of living fossil, and their skeletons must be very sound constructions. Unfortunately, we have no idea why nature arrived at these forms, although experience has taught us to expect that, for the radiolarians, they must be in some way beneficial.

Electron micrograph of a radiolarian skeleton.

Recent investigations of living radiolarians under an electron microscope have brought forth another astounding fact about their geometry. Each radiolarian extends many (sometimes hundreds) of very thin, elastic, and thoroughly straight threads (called *axopodes*), which are necessary for metabolism, through the tiny holes of the skeleton. The transportation of matter is carried out by the cell through extremely narrow tubes called *microtubuli*. Now, amazingly enough, these microtubuli are very regular. For example, some cross sections have shown a perfectly hexagonal array, like the honeycomb pattern. The hexagonally ordered microtubuli are connected by bridges that function as pumps.

Thus we see that nature seems to prefer order and regularity even in its tiniest structures. Today it seems to have been proved that tension forces at the surface of a cell only partly explain its shape; it is very likely that internal structures, such as microtubuli, are to a large extent responsible for cell shape.

Drawings of radiolarians by Ernst Haeckel.

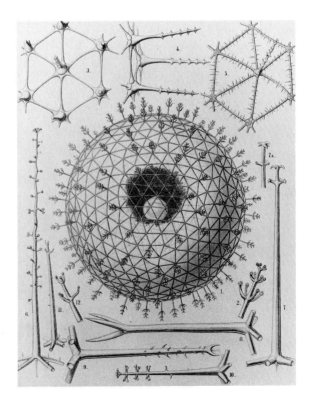

Cracks and Fissures

Fractures and fracture patterns arise often in nature. Mountain climbers dislike crevices, particularly when they are hidden under snow cover. There are cracks in the bark of an old tree or in the wooden beams that support the roof of your house. Of particular interest are polygonal fracture patterns, which may be seen in dried mud, in the varnish of old paintings, in ceramic glazes, and in enamel. We also find them in concrete, basalt, and limestone, in arid regions, and in frozen earth. Some patterns are formed of tiny tiles; others are made up of gigantic polygons. In the playas, the dry lakes of the Big Basin area of the western United States, aerial photographs of polygons between 100 and 300 feet wide have been made. The ground-ice wedges in Alaska and the Tundra polygons are well-known and often-described phenomena seen on the permafrost in polar regions.

Most scientists currently agree that the polygonal patterns seem to appear in materials that undergo volume changes because of drying, cooling, or both. The more cautious among them admit that we do not understand these processes at all well. Others see Bernoulli's principle

Crack formation by shrinking of plaque.

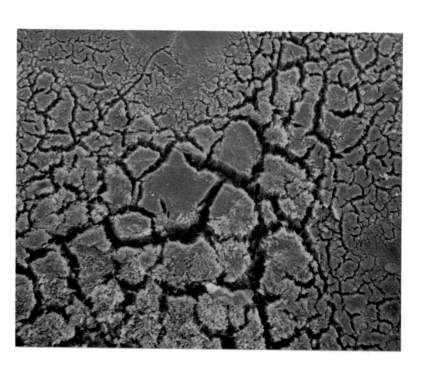

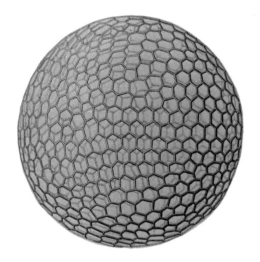

Pentagons and hexagons in a radiolarian frame.

of virtual work in action; yet the conclusions drawn from this principle differ from scientist to scientist. Some claim that the cracks have to intersect each other perpendicularly; others, that crack polygons must be pentagonal or hexagonal. In particular, the hexagon pattern, with the three-rayed vertices and the three 120° angles, is supposed to result from this mechanical principle. Not every plane domain can be covered by hexagonal tiles because Euler's formula imposes a restriction on potential tesselation (see page 114); so we usually find a few pentagons among many hexagons. Similarly, skeletons of radiolarians with mainly hexagonal cells are never purely hexagonal; we easily spot a few pentagons and heptagons.

We think that these "theoretical" conclusions are neither convincing nor well established, although they probably contain some truth. The theory of tearing and splitting of strongly viscous or brittle materials is not well developed. Moreover, we know that the most minute irregularities in a material might obviate all theoretical calculations. For example, it is rather difficult to tear a strip of paper with straight edges by pulling it at both ends, but a tiny notch at one edge makes the tearing easy.

It is well known that irregularities appear in most substances; hence it seems safe to assume that irregularities play an important role in the formation of cracks. The majority of earth fissures seem randomly distributed over the ground, and a new crack in a formerly uncracked area will develop in randomly formed zones of weakness in the ground. Moreover, fissures will not usually all appear at the same time. We find that at first only a few cracks develop. The tangential stress along the fissures in the crack zones is still quite formidable, whereas the perpendicular stress is released by the formation of the cracks. Therefore, secondary cracks will form perpendicularly to the greatest tension and thus tend to intersect the primary cracks at right angles. The ternary cracks will then meet the primary and secondary ones at right angles. In this way, a network of randomly distributed fissures that intersect perpendicularly will form. The history of the fractional pattern is therefore well documented. We can usually decide which fissure came earlier and which came later.

Unfortunately, the general situation is not as clear-cut. First, there are materials in which the cracks form strictly 120° angles. (A close inspection shows much narrower secondary fissures that meet the primary ones at a right angle.) Second, careful investigations have shown that the 90° angle, the 120° angle, and the 60° angle can appear. For example, of a large number of crack intersections measured at islands in the Mackenzie Delta, 80 percent were perpendicular; the 60°

Incipient post crack pattern on Kendall Island, N. W. T.

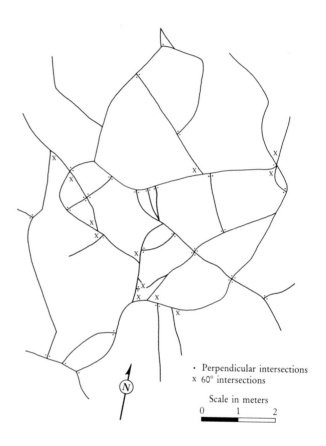

· Perpendicular intersections
x 60° intersections

Scale in meters

0   1   2

angle was the next most common, but very few triradial intersections with 120° angles were found (see the illustration above.)

There is a way to explain the 60° angles in terms of the principle of virtual work. Suppose that we assume that the frozen ground started to form a triradial array with 120° angles. Then unevenness of the frozen soil might have prevented the formation of the proper third ray.

If this were a sufficient explanation, the mechanical principle of crack formation could be saved. Accordingly, cracks would be formed either as single cracks (perpendicular to the direction of greatest tension), or as triple cracks with the 120° angles in a homogeneous material (yielding maximum release of stress with minimal strain), or else as the hybrid form, with the 60° angle caused by the "notch effect." Later cracks would be generated accordingly, but they would intersect former ones at right angles. We suggest that readers carefully observe natural cracks and formulate their own theories about them.

The Geometry of Crystals

Among the most-admired forms in nature are those of crystalline structures. Crystals, often radiating deep, rich colors, are as much sought after by collectors as studied by scientists.

A natural question to ask is whether the shapes of crystals can be explained by a variational principle. It is known that the form of a growing crystal is determined by several kinetic factors, such as the mechanism of transport of material, condensation, diffusion, and rates of chemical reactions. A complete understanding of surface structures is consequently difficult.

Crystals.

However, for small crystals or for crystals with small surface irregularities, it appears that a crystal's tendency to lower its free surface energy is the dominating factor in shape formation. We are therefore led to ask what shape a small crystal of *fixed* volume will assume if its free surface energy is to be a minimum. This reminds us of the isoperimetric problem in three dimensions, the solution of which is a sphere. In this case, the potential energy is proportional to the surface area, whereas the volume is fixed. The perfectly smooth and symmetric sphere is clearly quite different from crystalline structures. Nevertheless, when crystals are small, their shapes can be explained to some extent by a variational principle similar to that of the isoperimetric problem, and the remarkable difference in structure results from the difference in the corresponding potential energies.

A piecewise smooth body.

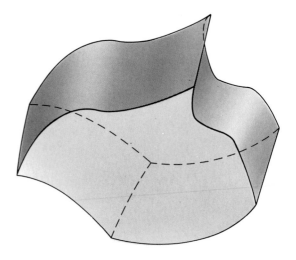

The mathematical problem can be formulated as follows. Consider a region in space bounded by a finite collection of pieces of smooth surfaces. Such bodies are called *piecewise smooth*. For almost every point on such a piecewise smooth surface, there will be a tangent plane. The surface energy for crystalline structures depends on the chemical nature of the specific crystal, and we shall assume that this energy depends only on the orientation of the tangent planes in space.

We then ask for the structure or shape that, for a fixed volume, has a minimum *total* surface energy. The remarkable discovery made by the crystallographer Georg Wulff in 1901 is that, given some further reasonable assumptions about the mathematical character of the surface energy, the following holds:

> For every given volume, there is a unique convex body whose boundary consists of planar faces, such that this boundary surface has less energy than does the boundary surface of any other piecewise smooth body of the same volume.

This theorem is remarkable in two ways. First, there is an infinite number of possible surface energies; nevertheless, for each such admissible energy, the unique minimum is a convex region bounded by planes. Second, unlike most problems in mathematics in which explicit solutions are impossible to find, the solution to our minimum problem, the optimal crystalline region, can be determined by a simple procedure known as the Wulff construction.

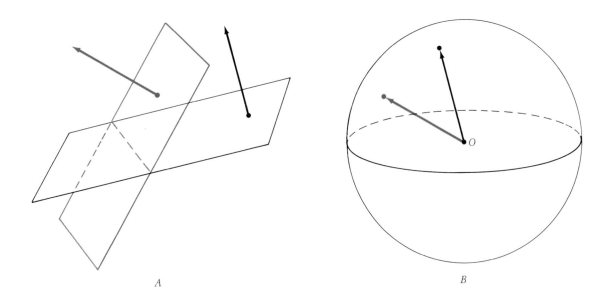

A   B

The directions normal to all planes form a sphere.

Wulff's construction is based on two assumptions. First, *the surface energy per unit area at any point on the surface depends only on the direction of the tangent plane to the surface at that point.* To each plane in space we can associate a "vector" (or arrow) of length one which is perpendicular to the plane. Such an arrow indicates the orientation of the plane in space, as shown in part A of the illustration above. We now fix a point O in space, and then without changing each arrow's direction we can transport them so that their tails are fixed to O. Thus each arrow is completely determined by its tip. The set of all such tips fills out a sphere in space, as shown in part B.

By this correspondence, we can think of the surface energy as a rule that assigns a positive number (the energy per unit area of a piecewise smooth body) to every point x on the sphere.

The second hypothesis on which Wulff's construction is based is: *For a given crystal, there are N distinct points $p_1, p_2, \ldots, p_N$ on the sphere of perpendicular directions and a "triangulation" of this sphere with these points as the vertices of the spherical triangles. The value $E(x)$ of the energy at any point x in the interior of a spherical triangle satisfies a certain inequality with respect to the vertices of the triangle in which x sits. If, for simplicity, we say that p_1, p_2, p_3 are the vertices of such a triangle, then,*

$$x = a_1 p_1 + a_2 p_2 + a_3 p_3$$

A triangulation of the sphere.

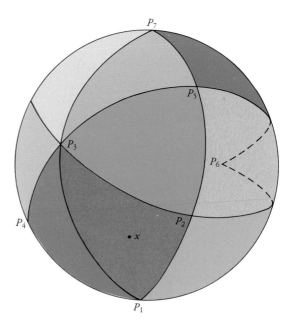

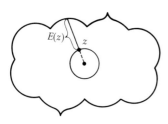

A cross section of the graph of a crystalline energy function.

for some positive numbers a_1, a_2, a_3. The assumption is that

$$E(x) > a_1 E(p_1) + a_2 E(p_2) + a_3 E(p_3).$$

If x lies on the edge of such a triangle, a similar inequality is assumed to hold. Because the energy E assigns positive values to a point on the sphere, we can think of plotting E as a "graph" over the sphere.

We obtain this graph as follows. For every point z on the sphere, we move outward, along the radial line through z, for a distance of $E(z)$ from z. Such graphs are difficult to visualize. A cross section, depicting what such a graph looks like in two dimensions, can be obtained by having the graph over the sphere intersect a plane, as shown at the left. We may now proceed with the construction of the crystalline shape with minimum possible total surface energy. For each vertex point p_i in the sphere, proceed outward from the center of the sphere along the radial line through p_i until you reach a point at a distance $E(p_i)$ from p_i. Draw the plane perpendicular to this radial line at this new point. The optimal shape is the bounded convex set determined by all these planes.

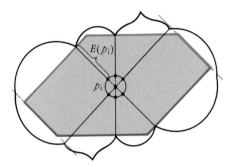

The Wulff construction.

A planar cross section of such a shape is depicted at the left. This shape, however, may not have the required volume. The crystalline body that solves the problem is obtained by rescaling this shape so that it encloses the desired volume. Wulff did not have a complete proof of this result. In 1914, Heinrich Liebmann showed that, if there is an equilibrium shape for the crystal, it must be the polyhedron obtained from the Wulff construction; so the question of existence was again left open. Finally, in 1944, Alexander Dinghas proved that any shape differing from that obtained by the Wulff construction has a higher total surface energy. Thus the beautiful and jagged crystalline form that we see in quartz and diamonds can, in some sense, be explained by minimum principles, as can the spherical and spheroidal forms that we see in planets, soap bubbles, and oil globules.

EPILOGUE

Dynamics and Motion

In the preceding chapters we have seen how variational principles have influenced both mathematical and physical thinking. We have restricted our attention mainly to physical systems *at rest*. However, the description of *motion* is equally important. We know that the Greeks had wondered about the shape of the trajectory of a stone thrown into the air and of the orbits of the planets. Yet the emphasis of Greek science was more on the geometric shape of the celestial paths and less on the *motion in time* along these orbits. We thus have followed the example set by the Greeks.

It is important to realize that the Greek scientists saw no relation between, for example, the motion of the planets and that of a falling stone. Such a connection had to wait until the seventeenth century, the Age of Newton, to be made. The foundations of *dynamics* (from the Greek *dýnamis*, "power" or "force"), the theory of motion caused by forces, were laid by Isaac Newton in his treatise *Philosophiae Naturalis Principia Mathematica*. The *Principia* consists of three books, the first of which deals with the motion of one or more bodies in empty space.

Book Two treats the motion of bodies in resisting media, such as fluids and air, and Book Three applies the Newtonian dynamics to the motion of the planets, to the theory of tides as caused by Sun and Moon, and to various other astronomical questions, such as the trajectories of comets, the motion of the Moon, and the shape of the Earth.

In the *Principia*, the entire program of modern mechanics is formulated, not only in content but also in style. Newton began like a mathematician by first giving definitions of the basic notions, such as

Isaac Newton (1642–1727).

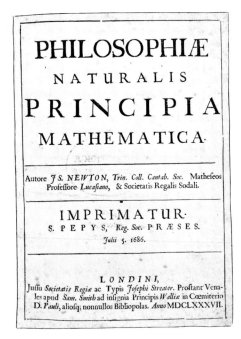

The frontispiece of a special copy of the *Principia*. This is the celebrated copy with marginal notes written by Leibniz, rediscovered by the Swiss historian of science E. A. Fellmann in 1969, and kept in the Bibliotheca Bodmeriana at Cologny, near Geneva, Switzerland.

mass and momentum, and then formulating three basic laws or axioms from which everything else was to follow:

FIRST LAW. Every body remains in its state of rest or uniform motion in the same direction unless it is compelled by impressed forces to change this state.

SECOND LAW. The change of motion is proportional to the impressed moving force and, secondly, it will occur along the straight line in which that force is impressed.

THIRD LAW. To an action there is always an equal and opposite reaction, or, the mutual actions of two bodies upon each other are equal and point in opposite directions.

Although Newton himself deviated from his rigorous approach (in the course of the discussions in his book, he employed undefined notions and applied hitherto unstated axioms) his axiomatic procedure made a strong and lasting impression on all later generations of mathematicians and physicists. Newton had achieved for dynamics what Euclid had achieved for geometry and Archimedes for statics.

Not everything in the *Principia* was new. For instance, the first law is nothing but Galileo's law of inertia, which Newton adopted as one of his axioms. A large part of Book One was taken from earlier writers, but it organized their knowledge systematically. Everything else is Newton's own contribution, and we can only admire how many difficult problems he dared to attack.

The three laws are only the formal framework of dynamics, and do not say anything about the nature of the acting forces. In fact, the second law has occasionally been considered tautological. If we want to apply the dynamical laws to concrete cases, we must specify the acting forces. Attraction is one of the basic forces, and Newton stated how this force acts:

Every particle of matter attracts every other particle with a force proportional to the mass of each, and inversely proportional to the square of the distance between them.

This is known as Newton's *universal law of gravitation.* (Actually, Newton nowhere formulated the law in this general form, but instead gave different versions in different places; these have been combined into the preceding statement.) He named the attractive force of masses *gravitas,* meaning heaviness or weight. Today we speak of *gravity* or *gravitation.*

In 1666, Newton derived the law of gravitation from Kepler's third law of planetary motion. Later he was able to show that, conversely, the law of gravitation and his three fundamental laws imply the three laws of Kepler. In particular, Newton proved that the orbit of a planet around the Sun is a conic section if the attractive force obeys the inverse-square law of gravitation. Thus Newton's philosophy of nature was a decisive step toward understanding physical phenomena by means of a mathematical model, toward the old Pythagorean dream of describing the world in terms of mathematics. Leibniz said of Newton, *"Taking mathematics from the beginning of the world to the time when Newton lived, what he had done was much the better half,"* and Lagrange commented, *"Newton was the greatest genius that ever existed, and the most fortunate, for we cannot more than once find a system of the world to establish."*

A century after the appearance of the *Principia,* Lagrange stated his general variational principle of dynamics; this was the mathematical formulation of the law of least action in mechanics.

Not everyone, however, was ready to accept Newton's ideas.

Johann Bernoulli found it difficult to believe in the concept of a force that acts through the vacuum of space over distances of even hundreds of millions of miles. He viewed this force as a concept *"revolting to minds unaccustomed to accepting any principle in physics save those which are incontestable and evident."*

Leibniz considered gravitation to be an incorporeal and inexplicable power, philosophically void.

Newton was also disturbed by questions about how this force acted, and he could give no explanation other than to say, *"I have not been able to deduce from phenomena the reason for these properties of gravitation, and I do not invent hypotheses; for anything which cannot be deduced from phenomena should be called an hypothesis."*

Moreover, in a letter to Richard Bentley, he wrote:

That gravity should be innate, inherent and essential to matter, so that one body may act upon another at a distance, through a vacuum, without the mediation of anything else by and through which their action may be conveyed from one to another, is to me so great an absurdity that I believe no man, who has in philosophical matters a competent faculty of thinking, can ever fall into it.

These and other difficulties of Newton's approach were met by Albert Einstein's *general theory of relativity,* which appeared in 1916 in his seminal paper "Die Grundlagen der allgemeinen Relativitätsthe-

Albert Einstein (1879–1955) at his desk in the Patent Office, Bern, 1905.

orie." When formulating his ideas, Einstein looked for a suitable mathematical setting, which, he found, had already been developed by Gauss, Riemann, and the two generations of geometers who followed them. Einstein devised the concept of a four-dimensional spacetime world that is not "flat" like the two- and three-dimensional spaces defined by the axioms of Euclid. The curvature of this world is generated by matter and energy. Near a large amount of matter, the amount of curvature of the four-dimensional world is large; far away from matter, it is close to zero. The exact relation between curvature, on the one hand, and matter and energy, on the other, is the content of Einstein's "field equations." Remarkably, as David Hilbert discovered, these equations follow from a variational principle.

In Einstein's theory, the concept of a force acting through great distances has been replaced by the curvature of the spacetime world. In order to elucidate Einstein's scheme, we shall present an oversimplified model that conveys some of his basic ideas. For this we represent space by a surface that we imagine as an originally flat trampoline (the vacuum state), which is at some point strongly deformed by the weight of a gigantic steel ball (the Sun). A tiny steel ball rolling on the trampoline is our planet Earth.

If we roll the small steel ball across the flat trampoline, it will travel in a straight-line path. However, if we now place the gigantic steel ball in the center, it will cause the trampoline to bend, even "far away" from the large ball. If we now give our little ball a push, it will no longer travel in a straight line, but in a curved path. The big ball affects the trajectory of the little ball by curving the space around it. With just the right push, the little ball might even orbit the big one for a while. This trampoline model explains how a large body could, by curving space, influence a small one over great distance.

A steel ball on a trampoline.

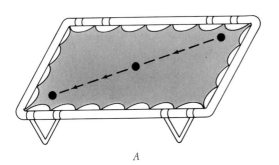

A

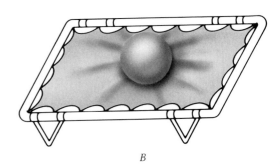

B

Max Planck (1858–1947).

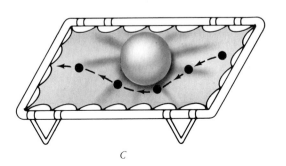

C

Moreover, in Einstein's curved world, light travels along *geodesics*. He predicted that light rays must bend if they pass through areas of large curvature, like the vicinity of the Sun. Usually it is impossible to observe light rays close to the bright Sun, but a solar eclipse provides a marvellous opportunity for such measurements. Two British expeditions to New Guinea (under Eddington and Cottingham) and to Sobral in northern Brazil used the solar eclipse of May 29, 1919, to observe whether light rays coming from stars and passing close to the Sun were bent. Both expeditions were able to confirm Einstein's prediction, and Eddington wrote:

Oh leave the Wise our measures to collate;
One thing, at least, is certain: LIGHT has WEIGHT.
One thing is certain, and the rest debate:
Light-rays, when near the Sun, DO NOT GO STRAIGHT.

We would like to end our account by quoting from a lecture given by Max Planck at the Berlin Academy, June 29, 1922, on "Leibniz day." After reminding his audience of Leibniz's personality, he drew attention to a very special work of the great scientist and philosopher:

the Theodicy . . . culminates with the statement that whatever occurs in our world, in the large as in the small, in nature as in spiritual life, is once and for all regulated by divine reason, and in such a way that our world is the best among all possible worlds.

Would Leibniz reaffirm this statement even today, in sight of the misery of the present time, in view of the bitter failure of many efforts not immediately aimed at material gain, in view of the undeniable fact that the imagined general harmony of people today seems to be further away from its realization than ever? No doubt, we should have to answer this question in the affirmative, even if we did not know that Leibniz never ceased to earnestly occupy himself until his last years despite an adverse fate and disappointments of all kinds, and we shall hardly err in assuming that it was exactly the Theodicy that gave him support and comfort in the most sorrowful days of his life. This once again is a touching example of the old truth that our most profound and most sacred principles are firmly rooted in our innermost soul, independent of experiences in the outer world.

Modern science, in particular under the influence of the development of the notion of causality, has moved far away from Leibniz's teleological point of view. Science has abandoned the assumption of a special, anticipating reason, and it considers each event in the natural and spiritual world, at least in principle, as reducible to prior states. But still we notice a fact, particularly in the most exact science, which, at least in this context, is most surprising. Present-day physics, as far as it is theoretically organized, is completely governed by a system of spacetime differential equations which state that each process in nature is totally determined by the events which occur in its immediate temporal and spatial neighborhood. This entire rich system of differential equations, though they differ in detail, since they refer to mechanical, electric, magnetic, and thermal processes, is now completely contained in a single theorem, in the principle of least action. This, in short, states that, of all possible processes, the only ones that actually occur are those that involve minimum expenditure of action. As we can see, only a short step is required to recognize in the preference for the smallest quantity of action the ruling of divine reason, and thus to discover a part of Leibniz's teleological ordering of the universe. The difference in the point of view is, as we see, by no means a difference in essence, but is solely a difference in interpretation, since the first restricts its view to the very small, whereas the other encompasses large distances in space and time. On this occasion every one has to decide for himself which point of view he thinks is the basic one, and must also ask which approach will eventually be more successful.

In present-day physics the principle of least action plays a relatively minor role. It does not quite fit into the framework of present theories. Of course, admittedly it is a correct statement; yet usually it serves not as the foundation of the theory, but as a true but dispensable appendix, because present theoretical physics is entirely tailored to the principle of infinitesimal local effects, and sees extension of considerations to larger spaces and times as unnecessary and uneconomical complication of the method of treatment. Physics hence is inclined to view the principle of least action more as a formal and accidental curiosity than as a pillar of physical knowledge.

Thus it has been even more surprising that this principle, originally viewed by Leibniz* and Maupertuis as a mechanical theorem,† was found by Hermann von Helmholtz to be valid, without any restriction, throughout the entire physics of his time. Recently, David Hilbert, by employing Hamilton's version of the theorem, has established it in Einstein's general theory of relativity. The more complicated circumstances become, the less likely it is that the dominance of such a simple law could be a mere accident. It is always a sure sign that an approach is incomplete if it cannot explain a commonly accepted, simple, and general relation. Our desire for comprehension will be satisfied only if every law that has been found valid has been understood in all its meaning and relevance, and has been integrated into the entire theoretical structure.

---

*Planck considered Leibniz to be the discoverer of the least-action principle.
†This statement of Planck is not quite correct, as can be seen from the account in Chapter 1.

REFERENCES AND FURTHER READING

Prologue

Ernst Haeckel (1834–1912), professor of zoology at Jena, Germany, from 1865 to 1909, was one of the first advocates of Darwinism in Germany. He participated in extended scientific excursions throughout the world and systematically investigated and described classes of primitive maritime fauna. His publications, famous for their illustrations, are bibliophilic rarities. A few that are relevant to this book are:

Reports of the Scientific Results of H.M.S. Challenger (London, 1881–1889). Haeckel's contribution to *Challenger: Report* was reprinted in 1966 (New York: Johnson Reprint Corp.).

Kunstformen der Natur (Leipzig: 1899–1904).

Das Protistenreich: eine populäre Übersicht über das Formengebiet der niedersten Lebewesen (Leipzig: 1878, Paris: 1880).

Die Radiolarien: eine Monographie (Berlin: part 1: 1862, parts 2 through 4: 1887–1888).

The following books are modern expositions on form and pattern in nature:

D'Arcy W. Thompson, *On Growth and Form* (Cambridge University Press, 1917; abridged edition by J. T. Bonner, 1961).

Peter S. Stevens, *Patterns in Nature* (Little, Brown, 1974).

Wolf Strache, *Forms and Patterns in Nature*, 2d ed. (Pantheon, 1973).

Stanislaw Ulam, "Patterns of Growth of Figures: Mathematical Aspects," in Gyorgy Kepes, ed., *Module, Proportion, Symmetry, Rhythm* (Braziller, 1966).

Frei Otto and collaborators: *Natürliche Konstruktionen* (Stuttgart: Deutsche Verlags-Anstalt, 1982).

The computer graphics of dynamical systems have been worked out by Heinz-Otto Peitgen and his collaborators at Bremen University. Expositions of their work can be found in:

Mathematics and Computing 1984, a calendar published by Springer-Verlag.

H. O. Peitgen, D. Saupe, and F. v. Haeseler, "Newton's Method and Julia Sets," in *The Mathematical Intelligencer*, Springer-Verlag.

Forschungsgruppe Komplexe Dynamik, eds. *Morphologie Komplexer Grenzen* (Bremen: H. O. Peitgen, P. H. Richter, 1984).

Chapter 1

The life and work of Maupertuis and his place in the history of science has been described by Pierre Brunet in two monographs:

Maupertuis: Étude biographique (Paris: Blanchard, 1929).

Maupertuis: L'Oeuvre et sa place dans la pensée scientifique et philosophique du XVIIIe siècle (Paris: Blanchard, 1929).

The second of these monographs lists Maupertuis's publications and publications of other authors related to Maupertuis's contributions. Moreover, we refer to Brunet's: *Étude historique sur la principe de la moindre action*, Paris, 1938.

A rich source of facts on the history of mathematics and physics in the seventeenth and eighteenth centuries is Leonhard Euler's *Collected Works* (*Opera Omnia*, ser. 1 through 4). Although more than seventy volumes have appeared, the editing is still in progress. Many first-rank mathematicians have added comments and historical remarks to the *Opera Omnia*.

The secondary and tertiary literature on Leibniz and Voltaire is so vast and so easily accessible that we will not list any of it here.

Newton's collected works have been published in this century. See *The Mathematical Papers of Isaac Newton*, D. T. Whiteside, ed. (Cambridge: 1967–1976). The first edition of *Philosophiae Naturalis Principia Mathematica* appeared in 1687, the second edition in 1713, and the third edition in 1725/26. All later editions appeared after Newton's death. An English translation by F. Cajori, *Mathematical Princi-*

ples of Natural Philosophy and the System of the World, was published by the University of California Press (Berkeley: 1934). The classic biography of Newton is David Brewster's *The Life of Sir Isaac Newton* (London: 1831), which in the enlarged second edition, became *Memoirs of the Life, Writings, and Discoveries of Sir Isaac Newton, two volumes* (Edinburgh: 1860). Further biographies of Newton have been written by F. Rosenberger (Leipzig, 1895), A. de Morgan (Chicago and London: 1914), L. T. Moore, *Isaac Newton: A Biography* (1934; available in a Dover reprint), and W. Stuckely (1936).

For the history of the calculus of variations see:

Leonhard Euler, *Opera Omnia*, ser. 1, vol. 24.

Herman H. Goldstine, *A History of the Calculus of Variations from the Seventeenth through the Nineteenth Century* (Springer-Verlag, 1980), which contains a select bibliography on the history of the calculus of variations.

The most important history of mathematics since the seventeenth century is the *Encyklopädie der mathematischen Wissenschaften*, which was edited by the academies of Göttingen, Leipzig, Munich, and Vienna, twenty-four volumes (Teubner, 1898–1934). Two older accounts that are still of interest are I. Todhunter, *A History of the Progress of the Calculus of Variations during the Nineteenth Century* (London: Macmillan, 1861), and R. Woodhouse, *A Treatise on Isoperimetrical Problems, and the Calculus of Variations* (Cambridge, England: Deighton, 1810); both of these have been reprinted by Chelsea Publications, New York.

Chapter 2

Despite extensive research on the history of mathematics, our knowledge of the mathematical sciences in antiquity is far from complete. As an example of a critical attitude toward historical research, we recommend Otto Neugebauer, *The Exact Sciences in Antiquity* (Princeton University Press, 1956).

As an introduction to the mathematics of the ancient Greeks, we suggest:

B. L. van der Waerden, *Science Awakening* (P. Noordhoff, 1954).

Morris Kline, *Mathematical Thought from Ancient to Modern Times* (Oxford University Press, 1972).

Morris Kline, *Mathematics in the Modern World: Readings from Scientific American* (W. H. Freeman and Company, 1968).

Of the scholarly accounts, we refer to:

Moritz Cantor, *Vorlesungen über Geschichte der Mathematik*, vol. 1 (Leipzig: 1894).

Thomas L. Heath, *A History of Greek Mathematics* (Oxford University Press, 1921).

H. G. Zeuthen, *Geschichte der Mathematik im Altertum und Mittelalter* (Copenhagen: 1896).

Basic translations of Euclid and Archimedes into English were provided by:

Thomas L. Heath, *The Thirteen Books of Euclid's Elements* (Cambridge: 1926).

Thomas L. Heath, *The Works of Archimedes with a Supplement: The Method of Archimedes, Recently Discovered by Heiberg* (Cambridge: 1897, 1912).

Both of these translations have been reprinted by Dover Publications, New York. An account of the life of Archimedes, of the history of his manuscripts and editions, and of the historical sources for Archimedes, as well as a new translation of Archimedes' works into English, has been provided by E. J. Dijksterhuis, *Archimedes* (Copenhagen: Ejnar Munksgaard, 1956). Here the reader can find further information on the defense of Syracuse and on the burning mirrors.

A very readable account of the history of astronomy, from the beginning until about 1900, was written by Arthur Berry, *A Short History of Astronomy* (London: John Murray, 1898). This book also contains a well-selected bibliography of astronomical literature before Einstein's theory of relativity.

Concerning the history of the isoperimetric problem, we refer to Helmuth Gericke, "Zur Geschichte des isoperimetrischen Problems," *Mathematische Semesterberichte* 29 (1982): 160–187.

Chapter 3

Heron's principle of light reflection, Schwarz's triangle problem, Steiner's problem, and related questions of the calculus of variations are treated in:

Hugo Steinhaus, *Mathematical Snapshots* (Oxford University Press, 1950).

Hans Rademacher and Otto Toeplitz, *Von Zahlen und Figuren* (Berlin: Springer, 1933).

Richard Courant and Herbert Robbins, *What Is Mathematics?* (Interscience, 1941; and more recent editions).

The first of these is an amusing and easily understood introduction to mathematical questions. The book by Courant and Robbins is the best introduction to mathematics that we know, but to use it one needs to know some basic mathematics.

For the solutions of Kakeya's problem, see A. S. Besicovitch, "On Kakeya's Problem and a Similar One," *Mathematische Zeitschrift* 27 (1927): 312–320.

The development of mathematics in the seventeenth and eighteenth centuries is extensively described in:

Moritz Cantor, *Vorlesungen über Geschichte der Mathematik,* four volumes (Leipzig: 1880–1898).

Publications in English are:

F. Cajori, *A History of Mathematics* (New York: 1984; plus various past editions).

D. E. Smith, *A History of Mathematics,* two volumes (Boston: 1923–1925; Dover reprint, 1958).

E. T. Bell, *The Development of Mathematics* (McGraw-Hill, 1945).

W. W. R. Ball, *A Short Account of the History of Mathematics* (Dover, 1960).

C. B. Boyer, *A History of Mathematics* (Wiley, 1968).

E. E. Kramer, *The Nature and Growth of Modern Mathematics* (Princeton University Press, 1981).

In addition we refer to:

Leonhard Euler 1707–1783: Beiträge zu Leben und Werk, Gedenkband des Kantons Basel-Stadt (Basel: Birkhäuser, 1983).

This memorial volume contains a complete bibliography of the secondary literature on Euler.

Concerning the infinitesimal calculus, sold by Johann Bernoulli to the Marquis de l'Hospital, we refer to: "Der Briefwechsel von Johann Bernoulli," vol. 1 (Basel Birkhäuser Verlag, 1955), pp. 123–157.

Chapter 4

One of the most influential books about the history of mechanics is Ernst Mach, *Die Mechanik in ihrer Entwicklung* (Prague: 1883; and many later editions). Many aspects of Mach's work have been strongly criticized, but, for a careful reader, the book is still very informative. One should read it together with Clifford Truesdell, *Essays in the History of Mathematics* (Springer-Verlag, 1968).

A survey of the history of the principles of mechanics was given by:

István Szabó, *Geschichte der mechanischen Prinzipien* (Basel and Stuttgart: Birkhäuser Verlag, 1977).

René Dugas, *Histoire de la mécanique* (Neuchatel: 1950).

R. Taton, ed., *Histoire générale de la science,* four volumes, (Paris: 1957).

The last treatise contains a good bibliography.

The mathematical theory of capillarity was founded by the French mathematician Pierre Simon Laplace, one of the great scientists of his time. His *Traité de mécanique céleste* is a cornerstone of celestial mechanics.

For the development of the mathematical theory of capillarity during this century, see Robert Finn, *Equilibrium Capillary Surfaces* (Springer-Verlag, forthcoming), and, for a popular introduction to the field, see the classic by C. V. Boys, *Soap Bubbles, Their Colours and the Forces Which Mold Them* (1911; Dover reprint, 1959).

Chapter 5

Giving full credit to the many mathematicians who have contributed to the theory of minimal surfaces is impossible because of lack of space. We will mention only some monographs on mimimal surfaces that provide a survey of the field. The theory of minimal surfaces, beginning with Lagrange's first paper (1760) and ending with papers published in 1974, is well described in the lectures of Johannes C. C. Nitsche: *Vorlesungen über Minimalflächen* (Berlin, Heidelberg, New York: Springer-Verlag, 1975).

Older and much less complete surveys can be found in:

T. Radó, "On the Problem of Plateau," in *Ergebnisse der Mathematik und ihrer Grenzgebiete* (Berlin: Springer-Verlag, 1933).

R. Courant, *Dirichlet's Principle, Conformal Mapping, and Minimal Surfaces* (Interscience, 1950).

R. Osserman, *A Survey of Minimal Surfaces* (Van Nostrand, 1969).

The basic ideas on how to use geometric measure theory in the theory of minimal surfaces can be found in F. Almgren, *Plateau's Problem: An Invitation to Varifold Geometry* (Benjamin, 1966). The fundamental monograph on geometric measure theory is H. Federer, *Geometrical Measure Theory* (Springer-Verlag, 1969). Some recent surveys are:

R. Böhme, "New Results on the Classical Problem of Plateau on the Existence on Many Solutions," *Séminaire Bourbaki* 579 (1981/1982).

A. Tromba, "On the Number of Simply Connected Minimal Surfaces Spanning a Curve," *Memoires of the American Mathematical Society* 12, 194 (1977).

W. Meeks, "Lectures on Plateau's Problem," *Escola de Geometria Differencial* (Univ. Fed. de Ceará, 1978).

We have (nearly) omitted the aspect of optimality that is closely related to the theory of regular configurations, such as mosaics, tilings, densest packings, clouds of spheres, and so forth. This attractive field contains marvellous problems, many of which are unsolved. Fortunately, we can refer to an excellent account: L. Fejes Tóth, *Reguläre Figuren* (Leipzig: Teubner, 1965), which is now available in an English translation.

On the optimality of the bee's honeycomb, see L. Fejes Tóth, "What the Bees Know and What They Do Not Know," *Bulletin of the American Mathematical Society* 70 (1964): 468–481.

The biographical material is taken from:

J. C. C. Nitsche, "Plateau's Problems and Their Modern Ramifications," *American Mathematical Monthly* 81(1974):945–968.

G. van der Mensbrugge, "Joseph Antoine Ferdinand Plateau, Nachruf," *Annuaire Academie Royale Science Bruxelles* 51(1885):389–473.

Minimal surfaces, soap bubbles, and other optimal constructions and their applications to architecture are discussed in:

Zugbeanspruchte Konstruktionen, Frei Otto, ed., two volumes (Frankfurt, Berlin: Ullstein Fachverlag, 1962 and 1966; an English translation is available).

Ludwig Glaeser, *The Work of Frei Otto* (New York: The Museum of Modern Art, 1972).

Frei Otto and collaborators, *Natürliche Konstruktionen* (Stuttgart: Deutsche Verlags-Anstalt, 1982).

The last book contains a selection of related literature.

The crystallographic point of view is emphasized in Peter Pearce, *Structure in Nature Is a Strategy for Design* (Chatsworth, Calif.: Synestructics, 1978).

Chapter 6

The classic on the isoperimetric problem is:

W. Blaschke, *Kreis und Kugel* (Berlin: W. de Gruyter, 1916; and later editions).

A survey on results concerning the isoperimetric problem can be found in:

T. Bonnesen and W. Fenchel, *Theorie der Konvexen Körper* (Berlin: Springer, 1934; reprinted by Chelsea Publications, New York, 1948).

Phenomena related to the classic isoperimetric problem were studied in the influential monograph by:

G. Pólya and G. Szegö, "Isoperimetric Inequalities in Mathematical Physics," *Annals of Mathematical Studies,* no. 27 (Princeton University Press, 1951).

A typical example of a generalized isoperimetric problem is the theorem about the plane domain of a given area that can support the largest sand pile. This result, as well as the theorem on the cross section of an elastic column with maximal torsional moment, has been proved by:

J. Leavitt and P. Unger, "Circle Supports of Largest Sand Pile," *Communications on Pure and Applied Mathematics* 15(1962):35–37.

Experiments on capillarity are described in:

J. Plateau, *Statique expérimentale et théorique des liquides soumis aux seules forces moléculaires,* two volumes (Paris: Gauthier-Villars, 1873).

G. Bakker, *Kapillarität und Oberflächenspannung, Handbuch der Physik,* vol. 6 (Akademie Verlagsgesellschaft, 1928).

Some of the results described in the section titled How to Take a Bath in a Spaceship can be found in:

P. Concus and R. Finn, "On Capillary Free Surfaces in the Absence of Gravity," *Acta Mathematica* 132(1974):177–198.

P. Concus and R. Finn, "On the Behavior of a Capillary Surface in a Wedge," *Proceedings of the National Academy of Sciences* 64(1969):292–299.

J. E. McDonald, "The Shape of Raindrops," *Scientific American*, February 1954, pp. 64–68.

Concerning the section titled Planets, Rotating Drops, and the Nuclei of Atoms, we refer to:

J.-L. Tassoul, *Theory of Rotating Stars* (Princeton University Press, 1978).

S. Chandrasekhar, "Ellipsoidal Figures of Equilibrium: An Historical Account, *Communications on Pure and Applied Mathematics* 20(1967):251–265; and *Ellipsoidal Figures of Equilibrium* (New Haven and London: 1969).

L. Lichtenstein, *Astronomie und Mathematik in ihrer Wechselwirkung* (Leipzig: S. Hirzel, 1923).

L. Lichtenstein, *Gleichgewichtsfiguren rotierender Flüssigkeiten* (Berlin: Springer, 1933).

W. S. Jardetzky, *Theory of Figures of Celestial Bodies* (Interscience, 1958).

W. J. Swiatecki, *The Rotating, Charged, or Gravitating Liquid Drop, and Problems in Nuclear Physics and Astronomy*, International Colloquium on Drops and Bubbles, Pasadena, August 28–30, 1974 (University of California, Lawrence Berkeley Laboratory, LBL 3363).

T. G. Wang, R. Tagg, L. Cammack, and A. Croonquist, "Nonaxisymmetric Shapes of a Rotating Drop in an Immiscible System," (Pasadena, Calif.: Jet Propulsion Laboratory).

On the section titled Cracks and Fissures, see:

L. I. Hewes, "A Theory of Surface Cracks in Mud and Lava and Resulting Geometrical Relations," *American Journal of Science* 246(1948):138–149.

R. Willden and D. R. Mabey, "Giant Desiccation Fissures on the Black Rock and Smoke Creek Deserts, Nevada," *Science* 133(1961)1359–1360.

A. L. Washburn, "Classification of Patterned Ground and Review of Suggested Origins," *Bulletin of the Geological Society of America* 67(1966):823–866.

J. T. Neal and W. S. Motts, "Recent Geomorphic Changes in Playas of the Western United States," *The Journal of Geology* 75(1967):511–525.

J. T. Neal, A. M. Langer, and P. F. Kerr, "Giant Desiccation Polygons of Great Basin Playas," *Bulletin of the Geological Society of America* 79(1968):69–90.

D. E. Kerfoot, "Thermal Contraction Cracks in an Arctic Tundra Environment," *Arctic* 25(1972):142–150.

On the section titled The Geometry of Crystals, see:

P. Curie, "Sur la formation des cristaux et sur les constantes capillaires de leurs differentes faces," *Bulletin de la société de minéralogistes français* 8(1885):145.

G. Wulff, "Zur Frage der Geschwindigkeit des Wachsthums und der Auflösung der Krystallflächen," *Zeitschrift für Krystallographie* 34(1901):449–530.

H. Liebmann, "Der Curie-Wulffsche Satz über Combinationsformen von Krystallen," *Zeitschrift für Krystallographie* 53(1914):171–177.

M. v. Laue, "Der Wulffsche Satz für die Gleichgewichtsform von Kristallen," *Zeitschrift für Kristallographie* 105(1943):124–133.

A. Dinghas, "Über einen geometrischen Satz von Wulff für die Gleichgewichtsform von Kristallen," *Zeitschrift für Kristallographie* 105(1944):304–314.

C. Herring, "Some Theorems on the Free Energies of Crystal Surfaces," *Physical Review* 82(1951):87–93.

J. E. Taylor, "Existence and Structure of Solutions to a Class of Nonelliptic Variational Problems," *Symposia Mathematica* 14(1974): 499–508, Istituto Nazionale di Alti Matematica.

Epilogue

The best survey of the development of mechanics, mathematical physics, and special relativity in the nineteenth century is:

Felix Klein, *Vorlesungen über die Entwicklung der Mathematik im 19. Jahrhundert*, two volumes (Berlin: Springer, 1926; 1927). This is available in English as *The Development of Mathematics in the Nineteenth Century* (Brookline, Mass.: Math Sci Press, 1979).

Further references:

J. L. Lagrange, *Mécanique analytique*, two volumes, 2d ed. (Paris: 1811; 1815).

C. G. J. Jacobi, *Vorlesungen über Dynamik*, 2d ed. (Berlin: G. Reimer, 1884).

H. Poincaré, *Sur la probleme des trois corps et les équations de la dynamique: Mémoire couronné du prix de S. M. le Roi Oscar II* (1889).

On relativity, see:

A. Einstein, *The Meaning of Relativity* (Princeton University Press, 1922; many reprints).

H. Weyl, *Space, Time, Matter* (Dover, 1922), translation from the German.

R. W. Clark, *Einstein: The Life and Times* (Avon Books, 1972).

C. Lanczos, *The Einstein Decade*, 1905-1915 (Academic Press, 1974).

SOURCES OF QUOTATIONS

Note: All translations are by the authors except where indicated.

page xii
Jonathan Swift, *Gulliver's Travels into Several Remote Nations of the World*, Chapter 2: "A Voyage to Laputa, Balnibarbi, Lluggnagg, Glubbdubdrib and Japan" (first published in 1726).

pages vi and vii
Translation by Helen and Hans Lewy from the German original "Korfs Verzauberung," which appeared in Christian Morgenstern, *Palmström* (Berlin: Verlag von Bruno Cassirer, 1922).

pages 1 and 32
Aristotle's, *Kleinere Schriften zur Physik und Metaphysik*, P. Gohlke and F. Schöningh, eds. (Paderborn, 1957), p. 124.

page 10
Arthur Waley's translation of Hsüan-Tsang's Chinese translation (about A.D. 660) of the Sanskrit *Mahāprajñapāramitā Sūtra*; from *Buddhist Texts through the Ages*, E. Conze, ed. (Oxford: Bruno Cassirer, 1954).

pages 10 and 12
Albert Einstein, "On the Generalized Theory of Gravitation," *Scientific American*, April 1950.

page 12
P. A. M. Dirac, "The Evolution of the Physicist's Picture of Nature," *Scientific American*, May 1963.

page 15
The Dante quotation is from an essay by R. W. Leonhardt in *Die Zeit*, March 1983.

pages 15, 16, 17, 25, and 26
Pierre-Louis Moreau de Maupertuis, "Les Lois du mouvement et du repos, déduites d'un principe de métaphysique," *Mémoires de l'Académie de Berlin*, 1746.

pages 19 and 20
Voltaire, *Candide or Optimism*, John Butt, trans. (Penguin Books, 1978).

page 29
Gauss quoting Shakespeare in W. Sartorius v. Waltershausen, *Gauss zum Gedächtnis* (Leipzig: Hirzel, 1856).

page 44
Johannes Kepler, *Harmonice mundi* (1619), as translated by M. Kline in *Mathematics and the Physical World* (New York: Thomas Y. Crowell, 1951).

page 57
G. H. Hardy, *A Mathematician's Apology* (Cambridge University Press, 1977), pp. 139–141.

page 59
Dorothy L. Sayers, *Have His Carcase*, Chapter 31: "The Evidence of the Haberdasher's Assistant" (New York: Avon Books, 1968), p. 312.

pages 81 and 155
Pappus, *Collectio*, Book 8. Adapted from E. J. Dijksterhuis, *Archimedes* (Copenhagen: E. Munksgaard, 1956), p. 299.

page 88
Hilaire Belloc, "The Waterbeetle," in *Cautionary Verses*, illustrated by B. T. B. Nicolas Bentley (New York: Knopf, 1959).

page 93
Richard Courant, *Dirichlet's Principle, Conformal Mapping, and Minimal Surfaces* (Interscience, 1950), p. 3.

page 102
Gaston Darboux, *Leçons sur la théorie générale des surfaces*, vol. 1 (Paris, 1914), p. 490.

pages 154 and 155
D'Arcy W. Thompson, *On Growth and Form* (Cambridge University Press, 1969), pp. 111, 114, and 115.

page 168
"Vous avez confirmé dans les lieux pleins d'ennui ce que Newton connu

sans sortir chez lui." The quotation is in S. Chandrasekhar, *Communications on Pure and Applied Mathematics,* 20(1967):251–265.

pages 174 and 175
The editor J. T. Bonner wrote in his "Introduction" to D'Arcy W. Thompson's *On Growth and Form* (p.vii): *"Of its importance there is no doubt, but we must agree with Medawar when he says that its considerable influence has been intangible and indirect."* The long

quotation is from p. 11 of *On Growth and Form.*

page 188
Isaac Newton, *Principia,* 3d ed. (London, 1726), pp.13–14. The Newton quotation is from A. Berry, *A Short History of Astronomy* (London: John Murray, 1898), p. 245.

page 189
The Leibniz and Lagrange passages are quoted from A. Berry, *A Short History of Astronomy* (London: John Murray, 1898), pp. 241–244.

page 189
Newton's letter to the theologian Richard Bentley is from M. Kline, *Mathematics: A Cultural Approach* (Addison Wesley, 1962), p. 393.

page 191
The Eddington quote is from R. W. Clark, *Einstein: The Life and Times* (Avon Books, 1972).

pages 191 and 192
Max Planck, *Akademie-Ansprachen* (Berlin: Akademie-Verlag, 1948), pp. 41–48.

SOURCES OF ILLUSTRATIONS

Escher Foundation, Haags
Gemeetenmuseum, The Hague.

pages 103, 104, and 110
Ortwin Wohlrab, Bonn.

pages 115 and 116
Institut für leichte Flächentragwerke,
Stuttgart, Professor Frei Otto.

pages 118, 119 (margin), 122, and 123 (top left)
Ortwin Wohlrab, Bonn.

pages 123 (bottom left) and 124 (bottom)
Institut für leichte Flächentragwerke,
Stuttgart, Professor Berthold Burckhardt.

page 125 (top)
After Imme Haubitz, Würzburg.

pages 126 and 127
Institut für leichte Flächentragwerke,
Stuttgart, Professor Frei Otto.

pages 128 and 129 (photographs)
Mathematisches Institut, Düsseldorf, Klaus
Steffen.

page 130
Eric Pitts.

pages 134 and 135 (top)
Alan Schoen.

pages 135 (bottom), 136, 137, 138, 139
(bottom), 140, 141, 143 (bottom)

Institut für leichte Flächentragwerke,
Stuttgart, Professor Frei Otto.

page 144
Steven Smale.

page 149
Etching by Albrecht Dürer.

page 150
Institut für wissenschaftliche Fotografie,
Schloss Weissenstein, Manfred P. Kage.

pages 152 (bottom) and 153 (top)
Tom Noddy (photographs by Bill
Reynolds, Santa Cruz).

pages 154 and 156 (part A)
Institut für leichte Flächentragwerke,
Stuttgart, Professor Frei Otto.

page 156 (parts B, C, and D)
After D'Arcy Thompson.

page 157
Institut für leichte Flächentragwerke,
Stuttgart, Professor Frei Otto.

page 158 (left)
Tom Noddy (photograph by Bill Reynolds,
Santa Cruz).

pages 158 (right), 159, and 160
Institut für leichte Flächentragwerke,
Stuttgart, Professor Frei Otto.

page 165 (left)
Paul Concus and Robert Finn.

page 172 (top)
After C. V. Boys.

page 172 (margin)
After T. G. Wang.

page 175
After D'Arcy Thompson.

pages 176 and 178
Institut für wissenschaftliche Fotografie,
Schloss Weissenstein, Manfred P. Kage.

page 179
After D'Arcy Thompson.

page 180
After Kerfoot, "Thermal construction
cracks. . .," *Arctic* **25**, 142–150 (1972).

page 181 (middle)
Steven Smale.

page 181 (bottom)
Egbert Brieskorn.

page 186
National Portrait Gallery, London.

page 188
Emil A. Fellman.

page 189
Hebrew University, Jerusalem.

page 191
Niedersächsische Staats-und
Universitätsbibliothek, Göttingen.

INDEX